Poems From Heaven

Poems From Heaven

Inspired by The Lord Jesus Christ

RUSSELL JAMES POSTIFF

To order additional copies of this book, contact:
Xlibris
1-888-795-4274
www.Xlibris.com
Orders@Xlibris.com
550032

Acknowledgments

I would like to thank my wife Irena for encouraging me to write a book containing some of my poems. I also am grateful for my friend Steve Miller for helping me hone some of the theology in a number of the poems and for some help with the editing. I also appreciate the patience that Xlibris showed me and the work they did on the book. Most of all I am deeply indebted to Christ for His great love and for inspiring this collection of poems.

In the morning feast on the Lord
Then throughout the day His riches will be your reward
Mull them over in your spirit and mind
Then you'll be like Christ in kind
They will saturate you inner man
According to His wise plan
The Scripture contains life and peace
Eating it, your anxiety will cease
You'll have the peace of Christ to arbitrate in you heart
Deciding all things from the start
You won't be at a loss of what to do
His guidance will shepherd you
You won't make choices on you own
But you'll hear His voice from His throne
Then you will properly grow
For His economy you now know

Don't take offense at every slight
To do so isn't right
For people the Lord does care
So treat them more than fair
Grace to me the Lord has shown
And good in me He has sown
So to others always be kind
Then love for them in Christ you'll find
In His image they are made
So honor to them must be paid
Faults we all have
Let your reaction be a healing salve
You might bring a lost soul to the King
If you're gentle in everything
This to the Lord is not small
So like Him care for one and all

Thanksgiving is much more than a duty
It is gratitude for Christ's love and beauty
At Him we get to gaze
For everlasting days
When our eyes feast upon Him
We'll know joy to the brim
Such pleasure it will bring
We'll forever of His glory sing
There could not be a better sight
Than this God-man Who is this world's Light
And our husband to be
Will always take good care of you and me
The only return that He asks
Is that in our love He could bask
Lord, this we'll gladly give
As we long in Your presence to forever live

I need not worry about the source of my next meal
For the Lord Jesus has marked me with His seal
Famished I won't be
Because Lord, I belong to Thee
You will keep me fed
As Scripture has truly said
This should not be my concern
But that Thy will I'd discern
And when it is known
I'd do it by the power of Your gracious throne
And if begging becomes my living
Your love You'll still be giving
But calamity
I don't want to bring on my family
So Lord, keep my dear wife and I
Following Thee until we die

Mammon, don't amass
No matter how much, it won't last
Use it for Christ's glory
To improve another's life story
Use it the gospel to spread
Or for a beggar to be well fed
Let your stewardship be right
Advance the kingdom of light
Care for your parents when they're old
Don't be in love with gold
To a friend be kind
Money won't bring peace of mind
Buy your dear spouse a gift
Don't let silver in a marriage bring a rift
Follow how the Lord says to spend
Then your treasure will be used to a good end

Jesus is good to you and me
And He always will be
We can rest on this fact
For in kindness He always shall act
We know this by the Holy Book
And by the path on earth He took
He never let a friend down
Even love for Judas was in Him found
Us He never shall forsake
For peace with us He did make
With His brothers He shares His heart
To His lovers revealing the deepest part
Lord, let me be such a one
Having intimacy with Thee, God's only Son
Never deserve You shall I
Or the fact that for me You did die
Because of the mercy You did show
My Savior I shall forever love and know

Equal to the Father is He
Christ the Lord God of glory
He is second to none
For He is the Almighty Son
There is nothing that He can't do
This I've known since I've been born anew
He laid the foundations of the earth
And died to give us new birth
He formed my spirit within
And rose from the dead again
He created a called race
By giving Abraham grace
He dwells in many a soul
He's the reason our lives are whole
How spectacular is our Lord and Friend
Of His reign there will be no end

Lord, why art Thou so good to me
It's unbelievable don't You see
In the Beloved I have such grace
Of sadness how can there be even a trace
That for me You would die
Brings a tear to my eye
And that company with me You keep
Speaking words so sweet and deep
More than amazed am I
How could Thee I ever defy
So Lord, my wild will tame
And cause my love as Yours to be the same
Let it be attached to only You
That with idols I'd have nothing to do
Lord, my faith please complete
And keep my countenance toward You ever sweet

Jesus is my freedom from sin
As I live out the righteousness within
For that I must hunger and thirst
Or else I might grow worse
Over me He keeps a watchful eye
That with my life I would not lie
I would live a life that is true
Faithful to the fact that I am born anew
His brothers must have the highest life
One that is pure and devoid of strife
For our Savior lived that way
Day after trying day
We can do no less
So us He would bless
Then confidence we will own
Never afraid to beseech His throne

It's good to intercede
And care for another's need
But Christ we must love above all
Not just to rescue those of the Fall
This is an important duty
But don't lose sight of Christ's beauty
His care for the lost is great
And He wants to change their fate
But He also wants brothers who love Him
Not just filled with works to the brim
So spend much time with your Friend
From the day's beginning to its end
Let pleasant thoughts of Him fill your mind
Always treating Christ Jesus kind
For He is your reason for living
So great attention to Him you ought to be giving

For people I must pray
If I want them to know Christ someday
For their destiny I care
More often the Savior I must share
That Christ too would be theirs
Not to be tares
A lovely relationship they would have
Knowing Jesus as a comforting salve
Then they too the gospel would spread
Others to be well fed
For Christ has commissioned us all
To tell others about the name on which to call
What better occupation could there be
Than to preach salvation is for free
But it cost our Lord His life
To end the cause of strife
So let us do our job
Our neighbor, of grace not to rob

Intentional is my Lord
Passivity will not earn a great reward
Follow Christ with purpose in my heart
From procrastination depart
Do what He says in a timely way
After you devote some time to pray
When you hear His voice
Follow it as you rejoice
The more of His will you do
The greater will be the testimony that you're born anew
The world will take note and see
That you take Christ seriously
Perhaps their hearts will be drawn
And truth upon them will dawn
That Christ is the Savior sweet
Who their need for life can meet

It's the Lamb's life
That saves from strife
On my own, unpleasant I can be
Lord, that surely does not glorify Thee
But if Christ Jesus is my supply
I express my Savior on high
I can treat my fellowman kind
As salvation in Jesus I find
He alone the higher life can live
Into Him my will I give
This He will bless
For to self I said no, and to Christ I said yes
This is the proper way the Christ life to live each day
As we listen to what the Spirit does say
For Christ's words He brings to us
To follow the Savior thus

Always listen to the King
In eating, drinking, or any other thing
For Christ's glory all must be done
To fully magnify the Son
Know that He is in control
Informing the actions of your soul
Be careful of what you tell the Lord to do
Let your words be few
Wisely chose what you say
Learn to firstly pray
Honor Him you must
Of your life that is the thrust
In the universe He has first place
And He's the head of the human race
Your duty it must be
To love, serve, and praise Him continually

The Lord for us has done good things
With Christ salvation He brings
He is a Father tender
Telling us to My Son surrender
For He is the sinner's Friend
Loving us to the end
So please the Lamb with your life today
Show others that He is the way
Christ needs to be made known
There are others He wants to gather around His throne
He will not lose one
That's been chosen to believe in the Son
Our salvation is secure
In Christ it will forever endure
So on your pillow you can rest at night
Knowing Christ has banished perdition's fright

Why be afraid at all
When upon Jesus you can call
He'll come straightway
When to Him you pray
Troubled He wants not your heart
His peace He longs to impart
So relish time with the King
Learn more of His praises to sing
Many you can find
As in the Word you search His mind
There Christ makes all things known
His love and the glory of His throne
Not another minute waste
Know that the Lord has a good taste
And make it your aim each day
Lovely things about Him to say

The enemy a loser is
He's defeated by those Christ calls His
Greater is He Who is in me
Than the one in the world you see
The cross was the death blow
The enemy is in the lake of fire you know
A pure universe belongs to the Lord
By all the cleansing His blood does afford
For sin He cannot look upon
Robes of righteousness we have put on
Christ's will we're able to do
We have resurrection power since we were born anew
The Lord directs our life course
For He's our boundless source
And one day complete we shall be
To the praise of His glory

Love all of the world's people
Whether strong or feeble
They all have value to the Lamb
And are named by the Great I AM
He wants them in His family of life
To end their God-ward strife
They would repent and see
Jesus is complete Deity
They would give their allegiance to the Lord
With all the strength their hearts can afford
This decision Jesus would bless
As to His salvation they, Say yes
This the Lord's heart would thrill
For His church He wants to fill
When the last soul does believe
Then complete glory He shall receive

Don't gaze at the world at all
Don't just be like a person of the Fall
For to Christ we belong
He is our life and our song
The world will drag you down
Loving it shall earn the Lord's frown
Purposeful as a saint be
Pursuing the Lord faithfully
Make each day count
Drinking Christ as a living fount
Don't ignore the bread of life
With nutrition He is rife
As you practice feasting on Him
You'll know true pleasure to the brim
Then as a Christian you shall grow
And true meaning in life you will know

The Tree of Life to eat
Is God tasting sweet
He's our supply
To serve the Lord on high
He is food to man
To carry out His plan
Work is not His main goal
But the nourishment of spirit and soul
Rich enjoyment of Christ our Lord
Growth in life will afford
It is life, not duty
That is the real beauty
It is knowing the Lord's heart
His will to thee to impart
Not of our doing alone
But also hearing His voice from the throne
Then satisfied Jesus will be
For He's free to work Himself into thee

Perfect are God's ways toward me
He loves and blesses beyond degree
His motives are the best
In them I can rest
Never shall He harm
Why have any alarm
Suspicious I need not be
For Lord, there is no guile in Thee
For my growth He cares
I hear His shepherding in my prayers
And a Good Shepherd Christ surely is
How wisely He leads those who are His
So the blessed assurance have I
That to Jesus I can always draw nigh
And grow me He shall
So with Him in peace I can forever dwell

Don't believe the lie
Christ loves you, for thee He did die
Truth displaces error
Jesus cannot be any fairer
His countenance is the most tender
Just give Him your heart in surrender
He will bless that act
With good things your life will be packed
For broken Scripture cannot be
He is faithful to thee
Each step of faith you take
More to His love you shall awake
Until you know it full well
As in His presence you dwell
And the day soon shall be
When Christ returns for you and me

Jesus came to die
But He doesn't want you to cry
Sympathy you may feel
But it's your soul He wants to heal
Sorry for Himself He was not
Suffering was part of His lot
Bravely He endured
So our salvation could be secured
How we must exalt this Man
For He fulfilled His Father's plan
Qualified alone was He
Aren't you glad He came for you and me
So let us edify others
To make them our sisters and brothers
Not a drop of His precious blood was wasted
So salvation by all might be tasted

To plant a seed I must try
To tell others my Savior for them did die
Reject Him they may
But I still need to pray
Perhaps it will come about
Their understanding of life they may doubt
Then open their hearts may be
To believe in Thee
How glorious this I would find
They'd come to know Christ's mind
That toward them He always has love
Now it's revealed into their hearts from above
Embrace it they will
Joy their hearts to fill
Then so satisfied the Lord will be
For He has changed their destiny

Listen to all the Lord says
Proving that I am one of His
His commands deny not
Prompt obedience must be my lot
That's the only way to prove my love
Following Christ above
Otherwise my love is a lie
And my actions my words would deny
Listening to His voice is not difficult at all
The Word says His yoke is easy I recall
So His yoke I will take up
Learning His will as with Jesus I sup
Follow through I shall
Telling others my Savior is swell
Then my heart will know peace
As all self-will does cease

More love for my brothers I must have
Like Jesus, be to them a healing salve
My brothers should be a treasure
Being with them always a pleasure
Christ takes note
If time to them we devote
Meeting needs
With kind deeds
In our hearts having true care
Our love with them to share
For to Christ they mean so much
So we must treat them with a gentle touch
Grace is the way
To show this tenderness today
Lord, thank You for this edifying word
I'm glad Thee I have heard

Of the Lamb I'm fond
I love our eternal bond
Forsake me He won't
Forget Him I don't
He's sweetly on my mind
It's a joy to think of Him I find
Many pleasant hours I spend in thought
Why me He has loved and bought
The answer I know
It pleases Him so
There's nothing in me
That's deserving of Thee
It's all made possible by grace
This brings a smile to my face
And when we stand toe to toe
That I love Him, I'll let Him know

Lord, You are my living water and my living bread
You're all that I'll ever need to be well fed
Who needs another source
When Jesus is my life and my course
Good and plenty is His taste
To sup with Him always make haste
Morning, noon, and night
Partaking of Him is always right
Let nothing stop the flow
Or inhibit you to grow
So earthly things don't crave
Or they will make you their slave
They can never compete
With your Christ so sweet
So why bother with them at all
Just spend your time on Jesus to call

Let the Lord decide all things
For wisdom into each situation He brings
It's His intention to make us grow
The best way Jesus does know
His ability question not
Shepherding is His lot
And you know He does it well
As the goodness in our lives does tell
Each circumstance He does arrange
Don't think your trials are strange
For your benefit He will use each one
To make thee like the Son
There might be anguish in the midst of it all
But on His name you still can call
Soon this life will end
Then time forever with Jesus we shall spend

It had to be that way
Only our Jesus the price could pay
I wish the Lord hadn't suffered so bad
But to see the travail of His soul He was glad
For many brothers He did gain
By His untold pain
Now enthroned in glory is He
Interceding unceasingly
This is such a pleasure to the Lamb
Bringing our cases before I AM
The Father answers each prayer
That more of Christ's image we would bear
His work He shall complete
By His intercession so sweet
The more we cooperate
The sooner Christ Jesus will be our Mate

Priceless is His presence
Just to enjoy His divine essence
For eternal days we shall
Our lives forever to be wonderfully swell
Conversations rich and sweet
With saints who in Christ are complete
Testimonies to share
How Jesus throughout our lives did care
Praising every aspect of our Lord's being
With so much more than being seen
Revelation will guide our days
Christ revealed in innumerable ways
No sin to muddle our vision
Never a saint held in derision
A completely satisfying life
And gone will be the word known as strife

Be vigilant to keep guard over my heart
That from Christ I would not depart
Departing is easy to do
If without grace you do not remain true
Let your love sacrificial be
Fully engaged Lord with Thee
A seed is in place
It needs to be nurtured with grace
It needs water and the sun
Or growth will not be properly done
The Spirit and the Lord's light
Will eliminate any blight
In myself, only a sinner am I
To the Lord's will I cannot comply
To the Lord I must turn
And for Him properly yearn
Then growth will occur
And by His life I shall endure

Care for what's on your wife's mind
Much wisdom there you may find
For she hears the Lord too
And may know just what to do
Years of experience she's had
Her choice just might make you glad
So follow through
If Jesus told her what He wants you to do
Be thankful you are blessed
With a mate who Jesus has confessed
It's not a small thing
The love and joy that she does bring
So really appreciate her
Show her love and respect for sure
Then your marriage will be strong
And to Jesus it will be a sweet song

Care for the truth, but do it in love
Following the way of your Savior above
Don't discredit another soul
For Christ paid for them in the whole
You may not think they're in the right
But be gentle, do not fight
Let your words be soft and kind
As you seek oneness in mind
Don't compromise on what is correct
But always seek peace with God's elect
Let the Lord decide what to say
Before you speak, please do pray
Wisdom you will find
And anger, your reason will not blind
Then you'll hear the Savior's voice
That in peace you made the right choice

A Friend of sinners is He
Forgiving believers completely
A grudge never holding
Once forgiven, never scolding
You'll see a smile on His face
And He'll favor thee with grace
Our God is so kind
We are pleasantly on His mind
For Christ has died
So with Him we could abide
A mingled life He wants us to live
Joy to Jesus that does give
To be one with man
Is the goal of His plan
Such a friendly Savior is He
Much gratitude have we

The Lord wants to be my All in all
He's the only One Who my heart can enthrall
I would not set my mind on lower things
Only my Savior satisfaction ever brings
At times I care for pleasure
My Lord I do not fully treasure
I know this is vain
Doing so, Christ I do not gain
At times food and drink I find
Occupy my mind
My belly they may fill
But I'm hungry and thirsty still
So I'll do what I know is true
And Lord Jesus, turn my heart to You
Then my joy will be restored
For Thee alone have I adored

Don't boast about my behavior
For any goodness is due to my Savior
Only a sinner am I
For truth, on Christ I must rely
I would be in bondage to sin
If I was not born again
At one time that was my life
Full of ugliness and strife
It was only because of that God-man
That the Lord changed my plan
So all praise to Jesus is due
In Him I'm a creation new
My old man is dead
I'm now Spirit-led
So Lord, I give You my love
As I treasure my Savior God above

Thy name is the sweetest on earth
Since I've experienced new birth
It's a joy to call
It's worship to my All in all
It lifts me up when I'm downcast
My sadness can no longer last
It brings peace when in distress
Oh how it does bless
In the universe it has the highest place
It is the source of all grace
The young and old can call it out
Even boys and girls can learn to shout
For Jesus' name there must be utmost respect
Your conscience it must affect
So take care of His name
And in your soul let it burn as a holy flame

Of my experience don't be proud
Not in silence nor out loud
For it's of the Lord's mercy
That He quenches me when I'm thirsty
The enjoyment of Christ that I've had
Always makes me glad
But self I must not exalt
That is a deadly fault
Christ is my source
That keeps me on course
To Him all glory is due
He's the One that made me and you
It is His working and willing
That His plan I am fulfilling
So no credit can I take
All praise is for the Son of Man's sake

Everything to me
Jesus surely must be
This most valuable soul
Wants me in the whole
Totally devoted to my Friend
My entire life on Him to spend
With each thing I do
I'd follow His wise counsel through
Success that would give
As Christ I live
For He's my firm foundation
As with Him I stay in relation
In tune my ears would stay
To listen to His voice as I pray
For this would issue in godly living
Praise to Him continually giving

Slow to anger is the Lamb
He is the patient I AM
For the Lord to us is sweet
With kindness us He does meet
A gentle rebuke He will give
So you'll know the way to live
His hand is not heavy
Of forgiveness there is a bevy
So be afraid not to approach His throne
His loving attention you do own
Tender words He will speak
Causing you, Him to seek
Christ's goodness you will know
And you'll tell others so
Just open your mouth in love
Sharing the good Lord above

Come to the Lamb and die
For self He did crucify
Don't let it rear its ugly head
By Christ be led
If you are a faithful one
You'll earn the praise of the Son
There is no better sound
Than to hear that in Christ you are found
You're learning how Christ is gained
And to love with love unfeigned
To you the Lord is precious and true
And you're delighted to be born anew
At the world you no longer gaze
In life you've come to a new phase
Your only joy is Christ our Lord
No other rival can your heart afford

Worldly things don't admire
Don't let them be your desire
They bring in enmity with God
He will gently correct you with His staff and rod
Stay bound to Christ in love
Always pleasing this One above
Fill you can He
To stay holy for Thee
The Lord gives much more pleasure
Than false worldly treasure
So why do I stray
When I've tasted His lovely way
I know it's indwelling sin
That I listen to this world's din
So Lord, please sanctify me
As I cooperate with Thee

A God nudge I enjoy so much
It is His guiding and loving touch
A nudge to turn to the left or right
Is much needed light
It saves from many a pitfall
I love the salvation of my All in all
I'm not left on my own
But have access to God's throne
I don't have to figure it all out
God's direction do not doubt
In the wisdom of Jesus my Lord
Is all the insight heaven can afford
He'll keep me on the right track
And I'll never have to look back
A better Counselor there cannot be
Lord Jesus, I owe it all to Thee

Our God is Christ the Lord
With all the awesomeness deity does afford
Nothing is too difficult for our King
He rules in everything
A bad decision He never has made
Even when our sins on Him were laid
He chose the cross
Quite deliberately, not by a coin toss
Regrets He has none
For our love He has won
That means the entire world to Him
Now He has satisfaction to the brim
The Father over Christ does boast
He's the same as the Lord of hosts
And for all eternity we shall see
The full scope of His deity

Christ is the Prince of Peace
So from all uneasiness you can cease
His supply chases it away
In His presence let your spirit stay
He has such cheer
It's so good with Him to be near
Concentrate on Him
And your light won't be dim
To those around it will shine
Glorifying this Savior of thine
To Him they may be drawn
The light on them to dawn
For if the Savior they truly see
Christians they might come to be
No more to be dry
But satisfied with Christ on high

Possible, Christ made salvation
Touching those in every nation
Many souls are turning
As the truth they are learning
For the truth sets you free
From sins ruling over thee
As Christ becomes enthroned within
Defeated is ugly sin
The way to love is opened up
Its source is with Jesus to sup
His supply is fine
Becoming like Him as you dine
Many sweet virtues you'll obtain
As you let Christ reign
And He'll lavish them on you
If His will you'll just do

For people I want to care
As I lift them up in prayer
To have a burden for their life
That Jesus would end their strife
They would come to know the Prince of Peace
Unbelief would cease
Life would be so swell
For in love with Christ they've fell
Their hearts would always stay that way
For eternal day
How love satisfies our King
To Him it's a most joyful thing
He wants it between sisters and brothers
To be lavished on others
The Savior always took this way
That's why over others He has such sway

Walk in love
That's the best way to express Christ above
Make an enemy a friend
As help to them you lend
But don't boast when you do
For the Lord expects it of you
A reward will be yours
This the Word assures
A brother always bless
With more, not less
Use kind words and kind deeds
Caring for their many needs
Together loud hallelujahs shout
The enemy to rout
And finish your course
With the Triune God as your only source

It is Christ that I love
This One gentle like the dove
He is my abode
As I travel life's road
He eases each trial
As I see His loving and compassionate smile
With these I shall grow
And blossom one day I know
One day I shall be just like Him
That will give us both joy to the brim
In the meantime suffering I find
I must be steadfast in mind
If I endure
My reward is sure
So press on I shall do
Until in person, Lord, I see You

He paid the price to live in me
He thought it worthwhile you see
In His presence I can dwell
For in love with me He fell
I deserve Him not in the least
But Christ has become my feast
He is the joy and rejoicing of my heart
From this life I will not depart
He wills and works in me
So conformed to Christ I'd be
A lifelong process this I find
As He renews my mind
Time is the key
For real growth you see
So patience I will find
In my Lord so kind

For the gift of righteousness I'm glad
When Christ sees me, He's no longer mad
Now I have His gentle touch
And He has blessed me so much
A wife that is a dream
Who with love does teem
A church full of life
With very little strife
A Bible to read
Growing the implanted seed
In Christ, a caring Friend
Whose shepherding will never end
A Life Tree to eat
With which nothing else can compete
An eternity with so much bliss
My Savior, in love I shall forever kiss

My incredible Friend
Our love shall never end
You placed it in my heart
When our relationship did start
I'm learning to care more for Thee
As Your loveliness I see
A precious journey is this
One that knows much bliss
Jesus, Thy name to me is so dear
I call on it, Thee to be near
Amazing comfort I find
When You tell me what's on Your mind
Loving thoughts they are
Thy shepherding to carry me far
And Thy goodness shall never end
As together eternity we spend

Better I must learn to follow
Having a walk that is not at all hollow
Pleasing Christ my King
Is truly a good thing
For me He did all
It is a glory on Him to call
I will make it my aim to please the Lamb
To better know I AM
Having the knowledge of the Holy One
Results in a reveling in the Son
No longer with Him to fight
But walking in the light
My Savior knows best
So I must not put Him to the test
So if much chastising I don't want to see
Lord, I'll no longer offend Thee

Jesus stooped so low
So God we could know
He took on human form
And endured life's turbulent storm
He did not relinquish one day
But fully followed the Father's way
He sought not His own glory
Even though He is the Author of our story
He ministered life to man
According to His Father's plan
Never doing anything amiss
With love this broken world He did kiss
But to a cross we nailed Him
Insulting Christ to the brim
He still said, "Father forgive"
That's the glorious way He did live
Now with honor He is enthroned
And our hearts by Him are owned

I want to labor in love
As did my Savior Christ above
He had much toil and pain
But never once did He complain
The Father He loved to please
Even though for Him there was no ease
He had so much goodness and grace
But some from Him hid their face
He was treated bad
But He made His Father's heart glad
Even His faithful band of few
Didn't understand what He came to do
Among themselves they had contention
When their place in the kingdom they did mention
But Jesus handled it all well
By the many parables He did tell
So with such a wise and wonderful Lord
Let's do the best, this side of eternity can afford

Rest and don't worry
Peaceful is our Savior, never in a hurry
How He loves to calm our soul
As we realize He's in full control
Nothing on us can befall
That's not the will of our All in all
He can even use the bad
To eventually make our hearts glad
As we give all our cares to Him
Joy fills us to the brim
Confidence we have
That to our wounds He'll apply His healing salve
For troubling life can be
Lord, how we need Thee
Happy am I to have Jesus my Friend
Our Lover that the Father did send

Have a heart of rest
For Jesus, thee has blessed
He loves to do so
I hope this you fully know
The greatest blessing is this
That on that day, His love thee shall kiss
For when that reunion takes place
You'll be exceedingly glad you ran the Christian race
The more of Christ you gain
The sweeter will be the meaning of your pain
In eternity your light will really shine
If your love for Him is fine
Don't be reluctant to seek the prize
To see true joy in His eyes
For in love He gives you the chance
Your eternity to fully enhance

Lord, for problems I'd like to thank Thee
It's part of Your loving economy
They turn me to You
To see just what You can do
There is always a good resolution
I find that Thou art the real solution
Jesus knows that heartaches at times I have
It's then I know Thee as precious healing salve
Sometimes a trial may linger
But Lord, toward Thee may I never point a finger
For You've only been abundantly kind
Trials I must not overly mind
You work them all out for our good
May Your ways in truth be understood

Satisfied is our Lord
This His cross did afford
For His brothers He did gain
By His suffering of pain
This was the only way it could be
For Jesus to purchase thee
For my dear Savior, I wish there was another route
But the Father's plan was wise, no doubt
Fully submitted was our King
In His endurance of everything
Now the benefits He did reap
Many redeemed sheep
Now we follow His voice
As we hear Jesus rejoice
And because of His plenteous mercy
We are no longer thirsty

Unbelievers, the Lord Jesus they do need
In them He would like to plant a gospel seed
As over them the Spirit does toil
He longs for good soil
An opening in them He would like to create
Before it is too late
Fallow ground He would like to plow
Turning their hearts somehow
That the kinsman Redeemer they would receive
As into Jesus they believe
For harvest, the field is ready
Just keep your prayers and labor steady
Jesus will bless
If your love for Him you confess
So to this lost world go
Telling them of the wonders that you know

How time passes by
We need to desperately gain the Lord on high
Every moment to treasure
Christ as our pleasure
Always knowing that on Him we can depend
His faithfulness never shall end
Complete us He shall
In that day all will be well
Until that time arrives
Holy we must live our lives
Seasoned with much love
To match our Jesus above
Taking nothing for granted
But humbly receiving the Word implanted
The sincere milk to drink
But about righteousness also to think
If both we do
To our Savior we'll be true

He laid down His life for me
So from all pride and prejudice I'd be free
All of my fellowmen I'd love the same
So I'd experience no shame
Christ sees us through eyes of love
We all look the same to Him from above
He loves little children, black and white
And always does them right
He loves young and old
As in the Bible we are told
He loves the rich and poor
The cross for them He did endure
All encompassing is His love and care
With saint and sinner, all of it He does share
How I'd like to be like my King
His love to exhibit, His praise to sing

Learn to trust and obey
It will make pleasant Jesus' day
A cooperating heart is His desire
A child of God that's on fire
Obedience is the measure of our love
How well do we follow Christ above
A tender heart is a very fine thing
But doing God's will, joy to Him does bring
Take the Lord's commands as a delight
Do not put up a fight
To your love He will appeal
To see if your heart is real
The proof is in our deeds
Not in just reciting verses and creeds
Make your faith one of action
For that will give your words real traction
Always do what you say
Then your Savior will really listen to all that you pray

Don't despair of His will
In following there is a real thrill
You'll see souls won
As God's will is done
To Christ, just take captive each thought
If you are blood bought
No regrets shall you have
Following Him brings a healing salve
There is joy that is great
Don't wait until it is too late
Consecrate your life to Him
And your vision will not be dim
For His secrets He shall reveal
If you let Him have your life's steering wheel
Then enjoy the ride
With Christ, your faithful guide

Care for my fellowman
Don't just live for my own plan
For our Jesus always put others first
Longing to quench their thirst
For self He would not live
He was always thinking of more ways to give
How can one Man love so much
Strong, yet with a gentle touch
His humanity was so pure
All for us and His Father He did endure
His deity was fine and sweet
In Himself He was complete
How could there be such a humble King
His own praises never to sing
But He is as real as can be
This the Bible does guarantee

Love people with every part of my heart
Treat them good from the start
With my mind
Think thoughts that are kind
With emotions sweet
Give care that is complete
With a will that is strong
Serve them all the day long
Keep my conscience clear
So I don't offend a soul dear
If these things I do
I'll be more like my Savior Jesus so true
For His heart He exercised each day
With kind actions and helpful words to pray
My Savior loved so well
That's why we all think He is so swell

People you ought to love
But don't forget your Savior above
He must have first place
This you can do by His grace
For the infinite gift that He gave
How can you not be His loving bondslave
You must pour out your all
On this One whose name you love to call
Lord, forgive me if my heart drifts away
And over me You don't always have full sway
A sinner still am I
But Thee, I don't want to ever deny
So Lord, fully capture my heart
Don't let Your mercies depart
I know I've been blessed to the uttermost
I love Thee Jesus, my Lord of hosts

My friends I want to be blessed
And by Jesus sweetly caressed
Trials they are going through
Even though they are born anew
The Lamb they love
Lord, keep them looking above
I hope You ease their pain
Don't let it be in vain
For their good, You can work it out
Don't let their hearts doubt
I believe coming are pleasant days
When You they will completely praise
In the meantime they must endure
And keep their hearts pure
Look to a reward they can
If they just keep following Your plan

Not everyone will believe
The truth they do not want to receive
In the Bible it is spelled out
By faith, believe with no doubt
The One true God gave us His Son
By Him all redemption was done
In person He is the same
This truth we must proclaim
Perhaps the Spirit will have a way
If for the hardened of heart we pray
The Lord desires none to perish
For lost souls He does cherish
I'd love to see Christ have mercy on others
To make them holy sisters and brothers
It is His sovereign choice
In His selection I can only rejoice

Soon Sunday morning will be here
When with the saints to Christ we'll draw near
There will be praise and song
Proclaiming that to Christ we belong
The piano will be played
Glorious music to be made
Our voices we will lift up
As upon Christ we sup
The truth we will declare
As over the hymns we share
Testimonies will be given
That our Savior we are livin'
The Word we will expound
Hopefully, in a way that is sound
And the Spirit will lead everyone
To more fully love God's Son

Peace in my Savior I've found
As with Him I spend time around
A peaceful word He will speak
Causing me Him to seek
He is the source of a soul calm
A true healing balm
This lesson I need to learn
One day at a time, His will to discern
If that I look past
My joy does not last
A weak individual am I
Too much pressure, then to Him I desperately cry
A Deliverer in Christ I find
Restoring peace of mind
Lord, what would I do without You
Happy days would be seldom and few

God wants to head up the universe in Him
So Christ will have preeminence to the brim
He alone is worthy of this lofty place
This King of grace
At God's right hand
Every soul must obey His command
A gentle Lord is He
Sweet in His deity
Now He reigns and rules
Love and compassion are His tools
In wisdom He is replete
The enemy He did defeat
He's waiting for the last soul to call
To make Jesus their All in all
Then the Lord will appear
This holy God Who to us is so dear

His presence I adore
I desire it more and more
It is sweet to my taste
To turn to my Jesus, time I will not waste
I'll make it my practice to be there
Enjoying the Christ for Whom I care
There my love will grow
That's the way my Savior to know
To experience the Word
Christ's voice must be heard
I savor its sound
I love His words profound
They are always a delight
And they give much light
So Lord, keep me forever near
And be my Friend so dear

Don't wander in my mind
With the Spirit come to dine
Let Him meet my need
And let Him lead
He knows how to love much better than I
Any coldness of heart He can rectify
He knows how to please the Lord
And to godly living move me toward
He is a Counselor too
Giving Jesus' point of view
He will disclose all the Lord says
To those who are His
In the truth He will cause us to walk
And fill our mouths with gracious talk
So give your being over to Him
To fill you to the brim

A friend loves at all times, day and night
To do so we must walk in the light
Receiving a supply from the Lamb
To be like I AM
There has never been a time when He didn't love me
The same I'd like to do you see
It's not in my natural man to do so
More of Christ's ways I need to know
As He transforms me by grace
His path laid out I will trace
It's one endued with love
With singleness like the eyes of a dove
It has only one goal in mind
To be like Christ in kind
His divine nature to display
In everything I do and say

Almighty God is He
Complete in His deity
There is nothing that Jesus cannot do
Especially for those born anew
He created the mountains and the sea
He made His blood the perfect plea
The heavens He stretched out
He'll save thee, His resurrection do not doubt
The foundation of the earth He laid
For your soul He has paid
He formed Adam out of the dust
He can surely win your trust
So put your faith in this good Man
And fulfill His eternal plan
Then reality you will know
As into Christ you grow

Israel, beloved of God
You He gently wants to guide with staff and rod
Through the wilderness thee He has led
As He fed you that heavenly bread
Water from the rock did flow
So His compassion you'd come to know
The soles of your shoes did not wear out
So His care you would not doubt
Your enemies He subdued
As your fears He soothed
Now to the nations a blessing you are
From your small beginnings you've come far
Now let the Messiah be your trust
Knowing Christ as Lord is a must
Then Jesus will be the peace you desire
As your hearts for Him are on fire

When you feel so sad
You think you'll never again be glad
Go to the Scripture and see
Jesus is your jubilee
No more in bondage are you
Life is now fresh and new
Don't forget you still have the Lord's name
For joy, "Lord Jesus," loudly proclaim
Let your heart sing a song
That to Christ you belong
As His brother you are His delight
Keep that thought in sight
How privileged are we
To approach the Lord's throne so free
So downcast don't stay
Let Jesus brighten your day

Jesus healed my heart
When His life He did impart
Many sad days had I
Didn't know that to Christ I could draw nigh
But sin kept me away
Day after day
Then one day me He drew
And wanted me to be born anew
My sin I saw
Enough to drop my jaw
I knew He had to be in control over me
That's when I bent the knee
That was the best decision I ever made
I'm so glad His blood for me has paid
Now others I tell
That salvation is more than swell

Don't wander in your mind
True love there you'll never find
If on Jesus our heart is set
Love you'll find, you bet
There is plenty there
And all the necessary care
A storehouse abundant it is
Dwelling in those who are His
Don't attempt to produce love on your own
Just lay down before Christ's throne
As you prostrate fall
You'll find Him as your All in all
As He fills you with His love
You'll know how good is God above
And with this firm foundation
You'll love the souls of every nation

God does not want to just straighten me out
He wants growth in life, no doubt
His element added to me
So Christ you can see
Christ wrought into all of my being
In ways to the eyes unseen
But Christ's fragrance to smell
That the work is going well
A reproduction to be made
As self to rest is laid
Growing up into my Head
As I am Spirit-led
This all done
To please God's Son
For when we are complete
The universe will be filled with love replete

Jesus is more than a love song
He's the One to Whom all glory does belong
He's a consummate King
Such reverence to Him we must bring
He's a Monarch with no competition
He was a Man on a mission
As a God-man He planned to die
To care for souls who in despair do cry
He let His precious blood be shed
As lost souls He fed
He had not one selfish thought
Glory for the Father He always sought
His enemies He did love
Such is our lovely Savior above
There is such mercy if in Him we believe
A greater gift we could never receive

Be restful in the Lord
With all the peace He can afford
Spend your time on Jesus dining
Your faith sweetly refining
Make it one that is strong and sure
One that any trial can endure
Make it supple yet strong
Fight the good fight all the day long
No lethargy would there be
Lord, in believing Thee
I'd have the full assurance in Your Word
That by faith I am heard
And your commands I can carry out
By your strengthening power, no doubt
This is the way in faith to live
Glory to the Lord God to give

Have fellowship sweet
With each dear saint you meet
Let there be abundant love
As you share Christ above
Let your words be gentle and kind
Speak what's on the Savior's mind
Show concern
That all, the Lord's lead would discern
The conversation He would guide
As together in Christ you abide
No harshness would there be
As each speaks in sobriety
It would be your aim
Christ to proclaim
Then built together we shall be
Living in unity

To follow the leading of Christ is good
The way to deal with people is then understood
The Lord never pushes a soul to believe
Even though their sin burdens He longs to relieve
He may take many years
To change their fears
To soften a heart takes time
To reveal Himself as the Lord sublime
The choice is up to Him
Even though He's full of mercy to the brim
Some Christ may never know
His way they don't want to go
It gives Christ a sad heart
That they would not let Him His life impart
But there are still many who love our Lord
With all the strength their hearts can afford

Starting another day
Doing it Jesus' way
Making all my doings a prayer
Having others in my care
Of my dear cousin Ann
Grow in life she can
Of Irena, my dear wife and friend
More time in Jesus' presence she can spend
More trust would be mine
Knowing just how much my Lord is so fine
Tomorrow when we travel back
No joy would we lack
Work again will start
But with grace it won't burden our heart
Lord, thank You for all You've done
You surely are God's wonderful Son

Pleasant my surroundings may be
But Lord, that's nothing compared to Thee
For Thou art my delight true
My joy is to be with You
Deep speaking to deep
My loving attention does keep
A charming God You are
The gentlest by far
Me You shall never harm
There is safety in Your arm
As Your love embraces my soul
I don't mind life's rugged toll
For I know in You
Someday troubles will be through
Meanwhile I'll endure
Following Thee for a reward that is sure

Luxurious living
Growth in life is not giving
Privations in life are not bad
In Christ they can make thee glad
He has much more in mind
That transformation of soul we'd find
Some pleasures are fine
But not on them to continually dine
Rather be a soldier for our Lord
Fighting His battle with one accord
For there is ground to gain
So from such ease refrain
Sacrifice learn
For God's will yearn
That is what counts in the end
The glorification of Christ our Friend

Freely love my Lord
By the supply He does afford
It's not just my own contrivance
But upon Him in reliance
The love that He feeds me
To His throne always leads me
There I reminisce
How He has given me such bliss
He has made my life better than I deserve
It's a joy Christ to serve
It's not just for a reward
But to show true love for my Lord
For I want my motives to be pure
For His glory I shall endure
My life to end in a good way
To be welcomed into eternal day

Food and drink will never fill
You'll be hungry and thirsty still
The secret is Christ the Lamb
Feasting on I AM that I AM
The lost, the world they savor
But that does them no favor
For they empty do remain
Nothing but futility do they gain
So better let us do each day
By taking Jesus as our life and way
If on Him we concentrate
This truth we can surely state
That good for food is our God
As to His table He leads us by His staff and rod
For Jesus as a feast is the best
And He is our eternal comfort and rest
There is no more to say
Except enjoy Him day by day

Jesus is sovereign over me
So in fear I need not be
Whatever trouble does befall
I can still run to my All in all
I know He'll calm my heart
And tell anxiety to depart
He watches over life's every detail
He does not want me to fail
To quit pressing on I must not do
For my years are too few
So the most of them I must make
Living for Jesus' sake
When overwhelmed I feel
I must come to Jesus for another meal
As on Him I feast
Troubles won't bother me in the least
So victory I shall pursue
And Lord Jesus, stay so close to You

What I need to do
Lord, is to come to You
Relying only on self must go
I must be a saint in the Spirit's flow
My liberation is He
In Christ He sets me free
The lesson of turning
I'm day by day learning
For in my spirit dwells a King
Supplying me with everything
I need not fret
If on my Jesus my heart is set
This truth never fails me
It's the Word's guarantee
But a method it I will not make
Rather do it in love for Jesus' sake

Excellent is our God
Benevolent with His staff and rod
To be good He doesn't have to try
Love can be seen in His eye
The expression on His face
Is one of tenderness and grace
There is strength in His arm
To save thee from any alarm
The feet that carried out His will
On a cross were made still
The hands that worked in a carpenter shop
On one Friday, nails did stop
The heart that with such love did beat
The enemy could not defeat
For on the third day
Arose our God to live and reign for aye

I'm safe in Jesus my Friend
All alarms He brings to an end
Defeated I can't be
If I follow Thee
He puts a hedge about me
As He does for each member of His Body
He keeps us ever one
In the glory of the Son
For we're the ones on His heart
Not for a moment does His care ever depart
The world pursues its gods
With us they are at odds
But it is our job to love
Showing them Christ above
Who knows how many we can gain
By sharing our Savior once slain
A compassionate God is He
So friend, I'll just pray He has mercy on thee

Greg, the Lord for you has come through
He did what He said He would do
A nice place to live
A job He graciously did give
He knew your concern
Christ you wanted to learn
Your desire is to please your Friend
To do so, to life's very end
He takes all this into account
As your trials He helps you surmount
Faithful you've been to Him
That's why your joy is now up to the brim
His love will never let you go
This truth in your heart do stow
Now look forward to Judgment Day
As you keep following His perfect way

Father, make me like the Son of Man
For that is Your wonderful plan
Every detail is Your concern
That to love like Christ for this I'd yearn
His words I would speak
Living like Him so meek
I'd master the art of grace
For each situation I face
Self I would not display
But my King each and every day
For if people see Him in me
Glorified Christ would be
For the more I age
I see Christ in history's every page
So to Jesus I'll remain true
What else can a Christian do

Learn the Lord God to trust
For faith in Jesus that is a must
Believe what He says He will do
You surely can, if you're born anew
Faith in your heart has been placed
In the Beloved you've been graced
So by this faith live
Each day to you the Lord does give
That's the only way to please our Friend
Doubt and unbelief bring to an end
In faith He answers prayer
As your burdens with Christ you share
A small thing faith is not
The amount you have, can be a little or a lot
But it is of paramount concern
For it's the unique way God's will to discern

Affliction the Lord will bring
But with love, to Him you must still sing
He wants you to grow
And yourself to better know
Our weaknesses trials declare
So we can come to Christ in prayer
He will sanctify them for our good
As His ways are understood
Don't let bitterness overtake thee
Let gratitude in your heart be
The dross He will consume
Don't let a cloud over you loom
Pass these days will
And His life in you He shall instill
So grateful be
He cares for your transformation you see

How I love to be called a Christian by my Lord
Those are the sweetest words His love can afford
To know I belong to Him
Fills me with joy and peace to the brim
To be a brother of Christ the King
Is a delightful and enriching thing
That He has set me apart
Makes me holy from the start
Sanctifying my disposition He will do
And make me uncompromising too
A righteous, loving life to live
As in gratitude, glory to Him I give
These are truly pleasant things
Joy to His heart it brings
And that is just what I want to do
For making me born anew

When melancholy is my heart
And all it seems is falling apart
To my Jesus I must run
And enjoy the love of God's dear Son
He knows my soul's deep pain
When trials are falling like rain
They hurt and press
Causing much duress
I might plead for the Lord to take them away
But rest in Me He does say
Your pain I will use to conform thee
So My image others will see
Your sorrow hurts Me too
But on this road I must lead you through
When your final destination you reach
You'll be glad for each lesson that I did teach

More than just to intercede
Or do a good deed
Christ I must love
Always seeking Him above
In my heart He deserves first place
This One Who gives so much grace
If not for His salvation
I'd be a hopeless part of Creation
But He filled my heart with belief
And from death I received relief
My constant companion is He
His goodness I truly see
The wonderful way He treats me
Into His arms I love to flee
My cup will run over for aye
And glory will fill each day

With my brothers be at peace
Any strife to Jesus release
None of us perfect is
Even though we are His
So be gracious to each one
Exemplifying Christ the Son
This brings pleasure to the Lamb
And lifts up the sweet I AM
All are in need of forgiveness you see
So critical we cannot be
That brings in the Lord's displeasure
When others we do not treasure
Many faults have I
This I cannot deny
So patient with others I will be
Just as Jesus is with me

Others I will not judge at all
When tempted, on Jesus I shall call
He will set me free
To truly love thee
That's the desire of my heart
To let all criticism depart
My King I want to display
Not to bring Him shame in any way
For all that He has done
I want my living to magnify the Son
Precious I find the Lamb
Fulfilling is I AM
So why have strife with others
Love them as my Christian sisters and brothers
Then I will see joy in my Savior's eyes
As up to His standards I rise

All eternity will be so good
Much better than can now be understood
Gone will be the blinders of sin
We'll fully have the mind of Christ then
To Christ we'll respond in love complete
Like Him, our countenance will always be sweet
The ravages of age will disappear
To Jesus we'll be fully near
Mature His Body will be
Fully expressing the Lord of glory
All natural disasters will be through
The earth will be wonderfully new
All mankind will know peace
War will truly cease
And Christ will reign in love from His throne
The most glorious position He will own

As a sinner, not better am I
Christ is my righteousness or else I must die
If not for His abundant mercy
I'd still be a wretch so thirsty
Nothing good dwells in me
Except Christ my reality
I flounder and fail each day
For forgiveness I need to pray
Jesus always grants pardon to me
Such kindness in Him I see
I thank Him for His covenant eternal
How He redeemed me form the infernal
Great love Him I owe
For all the lovingkindness on me He did bestow
And I know He deserves all of my being
As on Him I forever lean

More than compromise, you need grace
To put on marriage a lovely face
Grace can reduce friction to none
As both souls apply the Son
He knows all about peace
Causing you all strife to release
A marriage centered on Christ our Friend
All quibbling will end
The love that's in His heart
Into matrimony He can impart
Heavenly things will be
If both submit to Thee
For when Christ is the head of the home
Hearts from each other will not roam
And Christ can make marriage a dream come true
When both souls are born anew

Why such mercy on me Lord
With all the forgiveness heaven could afford
There was nothing in me
To deserve these riches you see
A scoundrel was I
Having no love for Christ on high
It was His good pleasure to save
This one who only sin did crave
I was headed for the pit
Until one glorious day I read the Holy Writ
I did an about face
And was saved by grace
Now my intention is to love and please the Lamb
With unbounded gratitude for I AM
If it wasn't for Christ my Friend
My life would have a frightening end

Jesus is Lord
This great truth the Bible does record
It is eternally true
He's sovereign over me and you
Out of His sight never are we
The good and bad He does see
Condemn us He does not
Forgiveness His blood has bought
To offend our Lord is never our desire
We'd rather serve Him as those on fire
For someday our Savior we shall meet
In worship we'll fall to His feet
For on hallowed ground we'll be
In the presence of this glorious Deity
Of our Christian journey this will be the peak
To be with the God Whom we seek

Look forward to tomorrow
Don't let anticipated problems give you sorrow
Jesus can solve them all
If upon Him you only call
Know that the Savior paves the way
To have victory each day
He is the sovereign King
Into His joy, you He wants to bring
If upon Him you will feast
He'll make the biggest trial like the least
Consider what Christ had to face
He did it all by His Father's grace
We can do the same
For we have the Lord's name
So fret no more
Just let your heart Jesus adore

Learn to trust the Lamb
There's no one better than I AM
A gentle soul is He
He'll set you at ease you see
In His presence is comfort and rest
At loving others He is the best
Why be afraid at all
He loves to hear you upon Him call
But in faith do so
His ways to know
Just as Moses did
Let the same of you be said
Like him, make your goal the Promised Land
There to conquer and make your stand
Let it be known that Christ does reign
Over the hills and plain
So bow the knee right now
To the One Who wore the thorns on His brow

There's repose for my weary soul
As all my cares onto Jesus I roll
Enumerate them I tend to do
Over my troubles to stew
This is not the Lord's way of peace
From such contemplation I must cease
Worry not does our Lord
This too I cannot afford
It eats away at my spiritual well being
Doing damage not at once all seen
From such musings I must refrain
Why the needless pain
Jesus carried every burden for me
He did it all on the cross you see
So as free as an eagle am I
Soaring to my Lord Jesus on high
There the air is clear
And with Jesus I love to be near!

Let my life be a glory to Thy name
Your true worth to proclaim
I would follow my King
Without knowing the reason for everything
But trust would be foremost
Pleasing the Lord of hosts
That would give the Lamb a smile
Not complaining about each trial
I would know that in His goodness Christ cares
All my pain and burdens He shares
He's not harsh at all
That's why I love on Him to call
Whenever I have great duress
His comforting words relieve my stress
When He says follow Me
I know blessings I will see
So why do otherwise
His wise ways I can only love and prize

I don't want an early grave
So in my eating I must behave
To live a long life
Void of strife
Obedience must be prime
All of the time
In a sense, my Lord Jesus is strict
He knows that sin, pain does inflict
So take a better route
Over His commands never pout
We know He has our best interests in mind
Know that He is only being kind
Our Lord to us is always good
Have you not yet this understood
Take the time to learn His ways
Then you will only be able to give Him praise

Be a good friend to my friend
Enjoyable times together to spend
Be generous with my time
As we fellowship around Christ sublime
We share in His glory
As we express Him with our life's story
Together we serve our King
Pleasure to Jesus to bring
Coordination among us brothers
To bring the Savior to others
They can then enter our joy
As their faith they employ
This is a most blessed way to live
True satisfaction it does give
And the church of Christ does grow
As more souls, our dear Lord come to know

Rich in my relationships be
Resurrection life will set me free
Love with the love of the Lord
Rich expression this does afford
He wants to be made known
Showing forth the glory of His throne
In His heart is such love
It's the most blessed thing above
As this love we share
It is the best way for others to care
It shall never run out
To a reward it is the surest route
Let your heart be at rest
By Christ's shepherding be blessed
Then your end will be so good
For Christ's ways you have understood

Jesus is never far away
He's in my spirit to stay
A glad feeling that is
Knowing I'm forever His
The Spirit's seal
To me means a great deal
Knowing that I'm marked out
Relieves any lingering doubt
Jesus is my Savior today
As He will be for aye
The enemy can't take that away
For I've been born anew since the day I did pray
Christ manifested Himself to me
So His salvation I could see
He took me at my word
When my voice of surrender He heard
Then He came in
To save my soul from sin

At another woman's beauty don't look
Before Christ wedding vows I took
My bride is all that I need
Gazing at her alone is a righteous deed
Christ together bonded us
To honor one another thus
Marriage exhibits the reality of Christ and the church
Matrimony ended my search
So honor my bride I will
My heart she still can thrill
I even think she's more beautiful now
I'm so glad I took that wedding vow
As I appreciate my wife
I exhibit the Lord's life
For He made us two one
Together to magnify God's Son

How amazing can it be
That the Lord lives in me
In me He wants to make His home
Free in every room to roam
Rearranging my life
Freeing it from all strife
Mending every relationship
With sweet love, me to equip
Growing my soul
To be truly whole
Calming my mind
In a way fully kind
A will that becomes strong
But to Christ does belong
And when the construction is done
How I'll truly be like God's Son

Since I've believed into His name
My life has not been the same
Many old attitudes are gone
And the Light on me did dawn
Love for the Savior is now mine
I care for the things of the divine
My sins now trouble me
From righteousness I don't want to be free
There is care for my fellowman
I want them all to know salvation's plan
I know the significance of life
There is so little strife with my wife
The world loses its allure
For Jesus, I want to endure
Bless You Lord, is all I can say
And work Yourself into me all the way

Refresh my Lord I shall do
Enjoy Him each day, for I'm born anew
Call on His name
His goodness proclaim
Love Him to the uttermost
Know in my heart that Jesus is the Lord of hosts
Share Him with others
Cherish my sisters and brothers
These things will satisfy my best Friend
And bring darkness to an end
His church hold dear
And each morning to Jesus draw near
Start my day in the Word
So His voice can be heard
Put all this into practice
Then Christ will have all the more bliss

Jesus is my good Friend
When in trouble, time with Him spend
A hand He will lend
For yourself you do not have to fend
You know He cares
And longs to answer your prayers
So His counsel seek
The wisdom of the King so meek
The problem He sees through
He knows the way to help the one born anew
He gives a shoulder on which to cry
Your faith just don't deny
Trust in the One Who has all power
To lift thee up this very hour
And that's what He will do
For He so very much loves you!

Learn to love what Christ does love
People below and angels above
His heart is set on man
They're the center of His plan
Redemption was foretold
In the Bible so bold
Genesis three fifteen
Surely sets the scene
Jesus fulfilled all that was said
When to the cross He was led
Why He had to die
Was because man believed the lie
But Jesus was the Truth that came
And put the enemy to shame
In God's eyes all is done
And in the church is the glory of the Son

Dear saint, I believe you love the
Lord with all of your heart
Even though deep trials of your life are a part
The Lord can use them to sanctify you
So you'll be like Christ through and through
When times seem rough
And you think life is too tough
On the arms of Jesus you can lean
A more tender Soul you've never seen
You know a wonderful Savior is He
Only good for you He wants to see
He can bless each day
As you take His perfect way
Like King David you can be
And by faith slay every enemy
For more than a conqueror are you
As by His strength you press through

My life's trials are not that bad
But often I find myself quite sad
A lack of faith I think it is
I must instead rejoice that I am His
For that affords the way
Into a brighter day
When I consider the trials of my Lord
Self-pity I cannot afford
A Man of sorrows was my King
But to the Father He still could sing
Such persecution He did endure
But His love toward man was always sure
Impossible this is for me
I need to lean on Thee
For if You're my supply
Others, grace I won't deny
That will be a blessing for Thee
And for fallen humanity

The Comforter is He
Shallow He never shall be
The depth of your sorrow He knows
Your pain into Christ flows
Each pound of sorrow He bears
Even if no one else cares
Never doubt His concern
His tender heart learn
People He has put around you
For they have loving feelings too
A help they can be
To lean on them be free
In the Spirit we are one
We must love like the Son
Then the Lamb will be praised
And the observing world will be amazed

Jesus is the Prince of Peace
So your worries to Him you can release
He will take care of them all
As upon His name you sweetly call
A troubled heart He does not want you to have
He wants to be your healing salve
So Lord, I gladly give my worries to Thee
As I watch You set me free
Restful becomes my heart
As all the stress does depart
In practice this is true
If I just come to You
You melt all my cares away
As I spend time with Jesus to pray
He's the lifter of my head
For by His grace I am well fed

Have you heard
In the Holy Word
He's Jehovah our God
Ruling with a righteous rod
Jesus is all these things and much more
The sweet Savior we adore
He's God fleshed out
Dear one, this do not doubt
The universe is in His control
As is the destiny of every soul
With His purpose align
Caring for things divine
Give full credence to the words He says
Long to become fully His
All that He has appointed for thee
From these things never flee
Such satisfaction this brings
To the King of kings

The more I obey
The better life will be in every way
Answered prayer will come first
Quenched will be all my thirst
Distraught I won't feel
With others in peace I will deal
My life will have more power
And my countenance won't be sour
More influence will be mine
To point people to the divine
Christ will have more pleasure in me
More of His wisdom I shall see
My love will properly grow
And much fruit my life will show
To the Lord no longer can I say no
To the Spirit, for His commands I will go

It's good to know there are people who care for the Jews
And want them to hear the Good News
They want them to be protected
Not by their enemies to be adversely affected
That Christ would keep them intact
And with mercy upon them act
They are precious to our Lord's heart
His life to them He longs to impart
When He does return
All Israel for Him will yearn
As Savior they will know Him
Filled with faith to the brim
A real resurrection that will be
Having the life of Thee
How I look forward to that day
When, "You are my brothers," I will say

Learn to trust in all that I do
That should be the state of those born anew
Perfect His wisdom is
So why not rest in it if you are His
This will lead to a more peaceful life
Devoid of so much troublesome strife
Remember, life I do not control
And I'm not sovereign over my soul
Everything I should defer to the Lamb
Trusting in the mercy of I AM
For Christ is perfect in all of His ways
If Him I follow, that is real praise
Sometimes I have a troubled mind
And rest I cannot find
But if I look to my King
I know once again my heart will sing

Young friends of mine
I'm glad you know the Divine
It's good to believe in your early years
That will save from sin and many fears
Learn to love Christ with all of your being
With growth in Christ in each other seen
Keep your fellowship kind
Edifying each other's mind
Meet with the saints each Lord's Day
Learn how to really pray
Make your life truly count
As any lukewarmness you surmount
For if you're on fire for the Lord
You'll look forward to a reward
Above all, keep your hearts pure
And all lifelong for Jesus endure

Learn to trust Jesus in all that I do
By His strength I can follow through
Whether a duty at home or work
By His grace, responsibility I must not shirk
While our Lord lived on this soil
For us He faithfully did toil
In His heart He did not complain
He did all His Father did ordain
Even though this included a rugged cross
Our Lord Jesus willingly suffered untold loss
A Kingdom He did gain
For all of His love and pain
Now He has perfect joy and rest
And He's looking for us to give Him our best
May this be every believer's desire
Living our lives on fire

Let all the earth proclaim His name
This Jesus, ever new, ever the same
In His character you can trust
For your peace you surely must
Perfect in all of His ways
As He'll be for eternal days
Precious He is to each saint
Of Him we have no complaint
For He always treats us so well
So in love with Him we've fell
And amazed are we
How our holy God is so lovely
With our sins He takes no pleasure
But He forgives with complete measure
Can you imagine anyone being better
Than this King Who has broken sin's ugly fetter
As for me, the answer is a resounding no!
More like Jesus I just want to grow

The Word my assurance 'tis
That I am forever His
He wants me to have blessed peace
That my union with Him will never cease
He'll give me the comforting thought
That with such precious blood I've been bought
He tells me that loved am I
By the Lord God on high
Nothing can sever this love
It's guaranteed by Christ above
No one can change His mind
That in me delight He would not find
His beloved am I
And my Beloved for me did die
So why let the troubles of life bind
When such a loving Friend in Jesus I find

O New Jerusalem come
For I love thee and then some
In that city to dwell
Where all things are well
Streets of gold
Where heavenly words are told
A city so pure
Where only love does endure
Christ at its center
Where into glory we enter
Where all the saints shall be
Praising Jesus eternally
No more sins to be made
Our countenance never to fade
But Christ we will shine out
Our destiny never to doubt

As on Mackinac Island I sit
I know the New Jerusalem is where I fit
This world is not my home
Over its land I roam
But when I plant my feet
On that golden street
Then I'll have true peace
And all searching shall cease
For I'll behold my King
It will be the most amazing thing
When I see His face
I'll be awed by grace
Those lovely eyes
Me shall forever prize
And I the same toward Him
My heart filled with love to the brim

Christ wants to gain our hearts
By the life He imparts
To give up our worldly ways
Our living to give Him genuine praise
The lust of the eyes
To no longer prize
Vain pleasure
To no longer treasure
Boastful pride
Fully laid aside
If these things we do
We'll appreciate our Lord anew
For He died to set men free
Not to keep the world company
So let us heed His call
To give Christ Jesus our all

Christ will exhaustively speak
Until I am lowly and meek
It takes many years to learn
All that for me Christ does yearn
A gentle soul I would be
Always loving my wife tenderly
Greatly caring for her and others
Especially my sisters and brothers
My life with them to share
Knowing that for me too they do care
My family I would love
Lifting them in prayer to God above
Generous I would always be
Just as my Jesus directs me
Then I'll be on my way
To receive praise from Christ on that day

Only You can fill me Lord
The world can only leave me dry and bored
When upon Thee I feast
I'm not empty in the least
I've never had a better meal
One that was truly real
You fill every nook and cranny
You watch over me better than the best nanny
For family we are
Your heart from me never is far
I'm learning how tender Your heart does sound
Such compassion in it is found
I'd love to be the same as Thee
Lord, work Yourself more into me
I crave that day when it comes about
That I'm Your brother no one can doubt

Genuine love is my desire true
For those born anew
Whether family or friend
I'd love them no end
For souls I don't know
My love for them would grow
For Christ loves every man, woman, and child
In a manner so tender and mild
To be like Him I would
This Christ Who alone is so good
Eternity long He's been that way
And that's just how He'll stay
In every facet His love does shine
As only can the divine
How blessed am I that it's mine
So I praise my Christ so fine

Jealous don't make my Lord
Give Him the first place His deity does afford
He loves me the most
Much better than can any of the hosts
Acknowledge this I must do
Caring for His feelings too
Often I hurt my Friend
The wrong message to Christ I send
Lord, change my ways
So I properly love Thee all of my days
I never want to hurt Thee again
But Lord, You know my sin
For forgiveness I'm grateful all the more
Lord, for this, Thee I do adore
Lord, make my heart more sensitive to Thee
That your point of view I'd always see

The Lord Jesus is my peace
For His reign will never cease
Off of me He'll never take His eye
And He'll always hear the sound of my cry
As He organizes my days
My mouth can only be full of His praise
Self does not know what to do
Unless Lord, it fellowships with You
I am grateful for each command
For it brings me deeper into the good land
The more I obey
The more delightful is my day
Of Your wisdom I'm discovering its soundness
And that its height is boundless
This has taken many years to see
But now it's setting me free

Trust Jesus your Lord
By the good grace He does afford
No one more trustworthy can there be
In the Bible that's plain to see
Our Lord keeps His word
Of that you can be assured
Never is He weak
The best for you He does seek
So keep your eyes on Him
He'll watch over thee, soul and limb
Safely home He will lead
As He meets your every need
Like the Father is He
Glad-hearted with you to be
So whatever you do
Reject not this Jesus Who loves you

About my job I need not worry
Or let my heart be in an anxious flurry
Christ orchestrates it all
I only need more on Him to call
The divine supply is there
Along with the Christ Who does care
Overwhelmed I ought not to be
In Christ, life is not too much for me
The ability belongs to my Lord
The need He will meet by the grace He does afford
I need to learn to rest
On His gentle breast
How He can carry my soul
And fix not the part, but the whole
So relax can I
Enjoying my Lord on high

Bragging rights not have I
For I'll be a sinner until the day I die
But of Christ I can boast
Of sheer beauty He has the uttermost
I want to be a lover of my Lord
According to all He can afford
A sweeter heart for Him
Serving with all the strength of limb
Of a command never feeling bitter
And of life never being a quitter
But press on in His power
Overcoming each hour
That's the best way to live
Such praise to Christ it does give
So I'll make that my aim
A prize from my Lord to claim

How beautiful is Jesus my Lord
Adorned with all the goodness His love can afford
A lovely countenance on His face
Saturated with grace
A wonderful hue in His eyes
A wonder to prize
In them you can see great beauty
Bound by love not duty
His hands were that of a working Man
Laboring to carry out the Father's plan
He did not veer off course
For the Father was His source
He prayed many a night
Gaining God's insight
And He carried God's will out
With grace to complete the work, no doubt

Let my day begin with praise
A joyful noise to Him to raise
A song to sing
Glory to Jesus to bring
Clapping my hands
Rejoicing in His commands
Dancing on my feet
With joy that is sweet
A smile on my face
Pondering His amazing grace
Amazement never to cease
At the loveliness of the Prince of Peace
A sight for sore eyes is He
The beauty of His face to see
And the fineness of this Man
No one could ever plan

Circumcision is of the heart
From the externals depart
Let Christ have a deep work on your soul
To sanctify and make you whole
He sees things you cannot see
He knows how to deal with thee
The cross will affect
Your self that you erect
At the root the axe will be laid
And self of no effect will be made
This is certainly the goal
That self-will no longer take its toll
But Christ through us will shine
That we'd express the divine
Our destination to reach at last
If to the living One we hold fast

Wisdom has my wife
She can help inform my life
The Lord gave me a good mate
Just as Proverbs 31 does state
Early she rises
And diligence she prizes
She loves each dear saint
And from trials she does not faint
She knows how to prepare a feast
With ten courses at least
She's kind to my friends
Time with them she cheerfully spends
In grace she is growing
As more of the Word she is knowing
Many would consider me truly blessed
And for that I find happiness and rest

The world cannot share a part
For Christ's home must be my heart
It must be a comfortable place
Where the Lord can dispense His grace
He must have the rule in each room
And must not be stifled as if in a tomb
For Jesus has purchased me
My own I cannot be
He has the full right to be my King
All I can do is comply in everything
Then with Christ I'll have peace
And my striving will cease
To kick against the goads I must quit
And over trials not throw a fit
Then Christ I will gain
With much less turmoil and pain

O how the Lord so sweetly does forgive
So in His presence we can live
Nothing between us want I
So I can fully draw nigh
As His goodness I taste
Our time together I won't waste
But I'll lavish praise
On the One Who brightens my days
I know His desire is my heart
That He would fully have each part
My will must comply
My emotions I cannot stifle or deny
My mind must always think a kind thought
And be thankful I am blood bought
My conscience I will keep clear
So me He can steer
Then pleased my Jesus will be
For He now has all of me

In His presence I don't have to cower
For He loves me each and every hour
Gentleness He does display
As gracious words He does say
So why come to His presence in fright
When I see much kindness in sight
Learn about Christ what is true
With your heart you must not rue
For you have the oil of joy
This do employ
Then your countenance will not be sad
In this day you surely can be glad
For He has made it for you
A gift to those born anew
So happy is my case
As I gaze into my Lord's sweet face

Deep within is the desire
For Jesus to be on fire
Fear seems to hold me back
Perhaps faith I lack
Patient Jesus has been with me
But more fruit He wants to see
To glorify Him is the goal
As people should do from pole to pole
He is so high and lifted up
Yet He desires with us to sup
His love He does display
As He invites us to unceasingly pray
On Him we can lavish praise
But He wants our hearts all of our days
And the more of ourselves we give
The more we shall joyfully live
So waste not another day
To Jesus give yourself away

Jesus wants me to have joy in all that I do
That is the portion of those born anew
For our God is full of glee
This too in you He wants to see
He is not somber and forlorn
Even though against sin He does warn
But He is compassionate and does forgive
So in His presence we happily can live
This almost seems too good to be true
But in the Word it is in plain view
So embrace each day
To Christ to joyfully give yourself away
Then you shall not have a bad mood
For Jesus is your food
This is the Christian life
Full of joy, not strife

My soul life I don't want to love
Rather my Lord God above
Self must not get in the way
Homage to Christ I must pay
Worthy is He alone
To be exalted on a throne
To Christ I must give my all
Or else growth in life will stall
My own desires I must put aside
And by Christ's decisions abide
He is both God and King
My opinion is not everything
My thinking with His must align
And choose the life of His design
Then life will mesh
As I overcome the desires of my flesh

A chosen vessel you are
Your faith will carry you far
But discernment you must use
Or the enemy, you he shall abuse
Learn to take all to Christ in prayer
Your walk with Him share
He's the only One qualified to direct
His shepherding has the best effect
So entrust your soul to Him
Filling you with trust to the brim
He has your best interests in mind
To you He is only kind
This kindness will continue for aye
As you enjoy Jesus day be day
So make it your utmost aim
To love and cherish Christ and His name

My lessons I don't seem to learn
I forget Christ is the One for Whom I yearn
I've been filled with Him before
And Him I'm coming to adore
But worldly water I still pursue
When nothing good for me can it do
The Spirit then reminds me of my King
That to Him again I need to sing
This always lifts me up
As with Jesus I sweetly sup
It's hard to believe
I forget the Good News I did receive
But a fallen man am I
On Christ I don't always rely
So Lord, remind me once more
You're the richest and sweetest store

The wisdom of eternal years
Calms all of my fears
Such a Wonderful Counselor is He
Truth in Him I always see
I know His ways are best
So in His words I will rest
A solution never does He lack
And of me, He never loses track
If I happen to stray off course
I know the way back to my Source
I simply turn and call
For the help of my All in all
Jesus runs to me
For I have His attention you see
So life need not overwhelm
For our Lord is at the helm

Holy keep your ear
Listen in godly fear
Defile yourself do not
For the Lamb loves you a lot
With the movement of your eyes
The Lord's purity prize
He was a pious Man
Always living according to the Father's plan
Your heart always guard
Never letting it become hard
Out of it are the issues of life
Save it from all strife
Never let it consider sin
That does not fit those born again
Then when Jesus you see
You'll praise Him with a heart that is free

What a gracious God we have
His name is like a healing salve
It is precious to call on Him
It makes us overflowing to the brim
Others we can then touch
Loving them in the Lord much
Selfish we don't want to be
But in resurrection live out Thee
For weak is the old man
To carry out God's plan
But if our spirit is strong
We'll have the living for which Christ does long
Remember, great power He has toward us
We can accomplish what He says thus
So complacent let us not be
But have real zeal for Thee

Live a life that is holy
Relying on Christ so lowly
By the Spirit and Word He cures your soul
To make thee complete and whole
The antidote to sin
Is the operating Spirit within
The Scriptures He'll apply
So unrighteousness you can defy
As more living water you drink
The less into transgression you'll sink
This water cleanses and supplies
Freeing thee from the enemy's lies
For the Lord Jesus won the victory for us
When He died, sin's penalty to bust
But His resurrection frees
From sin's power and disease
So from just struggling cease
Holiness is in the Prince of Peace

The righteous shall reign
This Christ did ordain
Co-kings over the earth they'll be
Bringing Christ to the nations you see
There shall be multiplied peace
For the greatest to the least
Blessings will be everywhere
Such love we'll share
There will never be another worried mind
How we'll treat our fellowman so kind
Jesus will be expressed by all
Every soul on Him will joyfully call
Of living streams we'll drink
Of unbounded satisfaction we'll be on the brink
Just endure for a little more time
Then we'll be with our Savior sublime

For righteousness hunger and thirst
That's the way to put Jesus first
Do all things in the proper way
That is such an aid when you pray
Don't have a crooked heart
From ungodliness depart
Let the Lord guide
As you cling to His side
Make fellowship a priority
Staying under His authority
This leads to joy that is true
Which might be long overdue
But Christ can bring it about
His ability don't doubt
And in following the Spirit live
As love to Jesus you give

Always care for my brothers
Loving them above others
Let my concern genuine be
Expressing Christ's tender humanity
For family in Christ we are
Our hearts should never be far
Lift them up in real prayer
For their needs show great care
Eternity together we will spend
Our friendship never to end
In the Lord's heart it's always been
That for each other we would fend
As our lives we lead
For each other to Christ we'd plead
Then when our time here is through
We'll enter eternity with a reward too

Let my love shine through
Especially to my wife born anew
She is such a blessing to me
I want to treat her sweetly
When a favor she may need
With me she never should plead
But I'll be quick to respond
To strengthen our loving bond
For she is my soul's delight
With her I want to be right
The Lamb must still come first
Only He can satisfy my thirst
But with my bride
I want to remain side by side
Such privilege the Lord has granted me
To know a girl as beautiful as thee

When you've tried all the world's pleasure
Then you'll realize Jesus is your only real treasure
Empty the world will leave thee
Full of death and vanity
No promise can it keep
So over its offer don't lose any sleep
Turn your heart to the King
For a real reason to sing
The Lamb offers you His all
If you will only upon Jesus call
A false promise never does He give
Up to His word He will live
For all power has He
And He's so loving you see
So to the world turn your back
Then joy in Christ you'll never lack

Be filled with Christ the Lord
If you want all the riches heaven does afford
They are a spiritual balm
Keeping a troubled soul calm
They are full of radiance and joy
And are good for young and old, girl and boy
In nature they endure for aye
You can enjoy them whenever you pray
Just come to Christ the King
As over you He does sing
Speak your love to Him
Let it be plenty, not slim
Tell Him He means everything to you
And all for Jesus you would do
But remember, little is your power
You must lean on Him hour by hour

I want to be wine to cheer both God and man
That is a wonderful part of His plan
Sufferings I need to go through
That comes with being born anew
I need not be afraid
Of the life for me Christ has made
For it is the best it can be
Perfectly tailored for me
There won't be one trial too many
But to be sure, there will be plenty
Chastisement some of it is
But mainly it's because He loves those who are His
So do not faint when reproved
By Christ let your heart be moved
Then when you at last enter into glory
How pleased you'll be with your story

Praiseworthy is my sweet Friend
Loving Him the bitterness does end
Why be so harried
When to Him one day we'll be married
Learn to cast your cares
On the One Who His peace shares
He can overcome the most troublesome trial
And actually give thee a smile
Learn to make a real turn
And His presence never spurn
He is quick to give you grace
So with life you can keep pace
His peace is like a placid lake
Deep drinks of it you can take
So discouraged don't be
Jesus overcame the world for thee!

It is God Who wills and works for His good pleasure
This truth we all must treasure
To please Him we surely must strive
For in us He is alive
A plan He has made
Faith's tracks for us were laid
Walk in them by grace
To find your proper place
He will accomplish what He set out to do
In all those born anew
The cooperation He works into us
So we trust Him thus
We won't miss the mark
If to His voice we hark
He will remind us to obey
As Christ Jesus intercedes each day
So be at peace with the Lord's work
You know responsibility He never does shirk

It is the Lord Whom before I live
My best to Him I must give
He is the One Who views me
My best I want Jesus to see
For man I won't put on a show
Jesus my heart does know
Transparent I will be
Truthful to Thee
Hidden sins must not be mine
I confess them to the Divine
Turn from them I will do
This blessed soul who is born anew
A heart without guile
Will make my Jesus smile
So Lord, purify my heart
And let true righteousness start

Thy name is divine
I'm so glad it's mine
Upon it I can call
My soul to enthrall
Many problems in life have I
Your name soothes me, I cannot deny
When I'm in a low estate
I call and Jesus never is late
He shows up with good cheer
And I'm glad I can draw near
There the comfort is beyond measure
That's one reason Jesus I treasure
As in Christ I learn to rest
I find life at its best
Only He can make life make sense
So why get troubled and tense

Don't be dry
When you have a supply from on high
With the oil of joy you've been anointed
To belief you've been appointed
Plenteous in mercy is our Friend
A call on His name the despair will end
His watering will never fail
So why in spirit be frail
Exercise your right
To put depression to flight
For Jesus has bequeathed it to you
Dear one, who is born anew
His name is a healing word
The most blessed one ever heard
The next time you are feeling sad
Straightway turn to Him Who makes you glad

A disability a soul may have
They need love as a healing salve
Christ gives it through you and me
As our compassion they see
So let us make our love known
If His name we own
In our hearts offer up a prayer
That is a good way to care
Answer the Lord may
To make for them a better way
The Lord's heart goes out to all
Their problems are not at all small
He knows the burdens they carry
To be their Savior He just might tarry
Lord, reach them with Your mercy
So they'd no longer be counted with the thirsty

Since I've been born anew
The Lord's will I'm learning to do
At times I fail my Lord
But grace He still does afford
A perfect gentleman is He
Forgiveness He giveth to me
This glorious Being I can approach again
For I am cleansed of my sin
His ways I must better learn
As His plans I better discern
All things He works out for our good
But His glory must be understood
For our highest purpose is this
Exalting Christ with a heart filled with bliss
Lord, let this my passion be
As I love and care for Thee

When His children God sees
He says glory please
I have given them my all
So on My name they may call
And if they do so
In them I will grow
His goodness He wants us to know
And all the favor on us He does bestow
Amazed we will be
When we enter eternity
There it will be revealed
All the depth of the good that was concealed
The Lamb we will praise forevermore
And in all His fullness, Christ we'll fully adore
Jesus will be the finest word we know
And our love for Him we'll never outgrow

Rejoice, dear Christian, rejoice
The Lord hears your troubled voice
Plenteous in mercy is He
Comforting abundantly
Your problem is not bigger than Him
The One filled with wisdom to the brim
By His almighty power
He can conquer your dilemma this very hour
He might let it linger for a while
Behind your sadness let there be a joyful smile
Never abandon you shall He do
In your trial He won't let you stew
Your salvation He is working out
His methods do not doubt
For a mistake He will never make
His way with you just let Him take
Soon the work will be done
And you'll fully resemble Christ the Son

Strive against the Lord I must not
For headship is His lot
The universe Christ controls
And He's sovereign over the destiny of souls
Fortunately, mercy I've received
Accordingly I believed
The Father and the Son
The best for us have done
The Spirit made it real
And gave us His seal
Now Christ we are tasting
No time are we wasting
Each morning we come to His throne
For a supply from Christ the living stone
And this fills our days
With His mighty praise

When the Lord commands
Don't make your own demands
Follow through
On all He says to do
The Lord I am not
Sovereignty is His lot
My only job is to obey
But for strength I can pray
In obedience there is contentment sweet
Disobedience will only bring sorrow and defeat
Better than Jesus I do not know
But at times I act like it's so
This is arrogance at its worst
This will only cause me terrible thirst
So Lord, myself I must humble
Or over the Rock I will stumble

Tender is my Lord
He gives all the compassion His heart can afford
I need not be fearful of His ways
Rather for them I must give praise
He leads me into the everlasting way
As I follow Him day by day
For eternal life is mine
Given by blood divine
Why not trust to the max
And in service don't be lax
For the reward is much
Tender feeling this does touch
It's a matter of coming to the throne of grace
For a supply of courage, life to face
Then my Lord will lead me on
To a sweeter and brighter dawn

God loves people of all kinds
Precious them He finds
How He wants them all to be reconciled
By their sins no longer defiled
Their outward appearance is not His concern
But that His voice they would discern
That if upon them He does call
They would trust Christ as their All in all
He longs to have many children for His own
To adore the Triune God on His throne
To be the Lamb's bride
No more tears to be cried
With righteousness to be adorned
Not to neglect His salvation we are warned
And in the end to find
Eternal life spent with Christ always
on our heart and mind

Unto eternity, beautiful is Jesus our Lord
He has the sweetest countenance heaven could afford
Anything for you He would do
It included a rugged cross too
Brother He is not ashamed to call thee
So have the same feeling for He
When His Spirit speaks to thine
Follow what He says in a way loving and fine
This shows that Jesus you do love
As deserves your Savior above
For idle is all talk
If with Him you do not walk
Everyday follow the Spirit's lead
As truth to you He does feed
Then the deeds you do
Will count for eternity too

There is much singing in the glory
As the Triune God writes our story
He pens each line
Filling life with the divine
Each detail is His concern
Teaching us how for Him to yearn
He takes away our worry
Telling us don't be in a hurry
Turn your heart to Me, He will say
Spend some time just to pray
Love Me in the Son
For all I have done
Remember, coming back am I
Bringing a reward from on high
So Lord, I will make of You the most
Exalting Jesus, the Lord of hosts

Much more of Jesus I need
Not just doing a good deed
To more completely connect
His will on mine to have a stronger effect
He wishes that Him I would not ignore
Or close my heart's door
But open to Him I would stay
More over His will to fully pray
There is no need to fear
That which to Him is dear
For when He makes His position known
I must embrace it as my own
Sometimes faith I lack
This only holds me back
So Lord, boost my belief
As in Thee I find relief

When painful, living seems to be
I need to turn and call on Thee
My faith strengthen
And my endurance please lengthen
My sad moments are not a few
Refresh me with salvation's morning dew
My thirst let it slack
As to Thee I come back
Often I struggle on my own
Not quickly coming to Your throne
For that is the only place
To experience amazing grace
That You're patient I am glad
And that You're a loving Dad
Father, Your mercy I will always need
As on Your faithfulness I daily feed

Redeemed in His holy name
He has not left me the same
Sin no longer reigns in me
For in Christ I am free
Doubts about where with Him I stand
Are no longer out of hand
Our relationship is real
Love for Him I feel
It surely needs to grow
Better His heart I need to know
I wish my trust was more
But I greatly anticipate what's in store
I look forward to being with Him
When my seeing will no longer be dim
But now, by faith I must live
Love to Jesus to fully give

This wonderful Fountainhead
By us to death was bled
His only crime was love
Man could not see the heart of this Savior above
His flesh concealed a glory so bright
We didn't know He was a beautiful sight
We took Him as a mere creature
We didn't know His every hidden good feature
But the Father knew His heart
That He was a lowly King from the start
Christ His own would not seek
But He poured out His life for the sinful and weak
He counted the cost
And treasured us enough, Himself to be lost
To the Father He is a supreme delight
In our hearts, we know this is wonderfully right

Never once did our Lord grumble
He would not even cause the least of these to stumble
He had the greatest reason
Fallen man's blatant treason
We were made for our Maker
But of Him we became a forsaker
We took the enemy's side
No longer with Christ to abide
We committed sins so great
We deserved a dismal fate
But the Savior's heart is so full of love
He could not resist leaving His home above
So He took on the form of a slave
And faced a lonely grave
Then He came out on the other side
With the redeemed ever to abide

Care for Christ in my heart
Don't let love for Him depart
For all the love that He has shown
My heart He must own
Reluctant I ought not to be
When I see how well He cares for me
Not a day has gone by
When to Him He would not let me draw nigh
Knowing that perdition is not my lot
For with such precious blood I've been bought
This deserves an eternal ringing shout
His goodness to ever tout
O the wisdom of His way
How this Shepherd guides me every day
Lord, forgive me when I complain against Thee
For You cannot more wonderful ever be!

Christ is the best Friend I'll ever have
How He anoints my soul with healing salve
He knows when I hurt on the inside
He calls me with Him to sweetly abide
His comfort I enjoy so much
Just to have such a loving touch
He knows my weakness
How He comes to me in all meekness
Jesus I long to be close to
And to hear kind words, not a few
With His warm, tender heart
I don't want to ever be apart
Lord, show mercy to your brothers
I love how You are so mild like many mothers
When from this life I pass away
Stay ever near I pray

When people take the Lord's name in vain
From condemning them I must refrain
They are ignorant of the fact
That in grievous sin they do act
For them I must pray
That someday they would take the Lord's way
They have no understanding of how
great is Christ their Friend
Or how much Jesus they offend
In this condition man is born
Between good and evil he is torn
God's image we bear
But for righteousness we do not care
Unless the Lord our conscience does awake
That sin we must forsake
So Lord, I ask mercy from Thee
That lost man the truth would see

Don't love money or what it can buy
For that will not endear you to the Lord on high
Rather care for what matters most
Loving people and the Lord of hosts
That is God's prescription for a life that is fine
One that with Him can freely dine
Christ on your list should be first
As the One to quench your thirst
Material things have no value that is real
So affection for them do not feel
Christ must have His proper place
If you want Him to have a smile on His face
A patient God is He
Slowly setting you free
Take the time to grow
Then in the end, victory you shall know

Come to my Savior above
The One Who is complete love
Learn to express His heart
From the moment the day does start
When a stranger you see
Respect their value and humanity
Judgment don't pass
Your fellowman don't harass
Show the kindness of your King
Perhaps salvation you will bring
Remember, life can be difficult for them too
They need care and compassion from you
People, the enemy they are not
But souls, the best for them should be sought
So let your concern be true
In all that you do

A person's ability
Does not affect their nobility
For the image of God they bear
How Jesus for them does care
For all He has died
He cares for what's on the inside
Do you love Him with all of your heart
Are you willing with possessions to part
Is His purpose on your mind
Do you treat your fellowman kind
These are the questions that are real
How about Christ do you feel
Don't let your heart be aloof
He loves you with certain proof
So make Him your King
And love the real thing

How encouraging the Lord's goodness is
How He lavishes it on those who are His
But He displays it to the whole human race
He surely loves to give grace
If you are called by His name
In your heart burns a loving flame
Christ you long to exalt
This perfect God without fault
He's also known as the Son of Man
The One Who died according to God's plan
He alone was qualified
"It is finished," to have cried
The enmity He cleared up
Now man with God can sup
Our life should now praise the Lamb alone
The God of life on His throne

I've found what I'm looking for
It's all wrapped up in the Christ I adore
His heart to know
Is the best way to go
There is delightful satisfaction
Leading to godly action
There is much food for thought
Considering the precious blood by
which I've been bought
There are days filled with tender love
Worshipping my Savior God above
There is the privilege of praise
And learning Jesus' ways
There is work to do
Seeing souls being born anew
In Christ I'll have all that I'll ever need
As my Savior, in love, forever does lead

All Three of the Trinity
Are in love with you and me
The Second died
So with God we could abide
The Spirit did flow
So Jesus we could know
The Father chose
And truth in us He sows
How involved are all Three
While maintaining Their unity
Separate Them we must not
For oneness is God's lot
They all equally desire our love
That we'd be attracted to things above
In eternity Them we will see
As into Jesus' arms we flee

How indebted I am to the saints of old
Who lived out Christ so bold
Such wonderful stories are told
Of flock and fold
In Hebrews chapter eleven
Are saints who overcame leaven
A godly life they did live
Glory to God to give
A brave heart they displayed
Even as they were slayed
Deliverance they would not accept
No unbelief into them had crept
So like them we'll do the same
For we too have Jesus' name
So from all fear turn away
And earn a reward in that day

Our God is in control of the rain
And every other thing that He does ordain
In Him we can rest
Knowing that He does what is best
Trusting Him feels so sweet
That our every need He does meet
It gives Him great pleasure
If of faith we have a good measure
That gives Him the ground to work in our life
Rescuing us from all strife
For He wants a Body at peace
Where all contention does cease
Brother loving brother
In deed and truth caring for one another
Our faith living out
So the world, our Christ will not doubt

The church is not mine
It belongs to the Lord divine
But of it He lets me be a part
And He wants it to capture my heart
That each member I would love
To please my Jesus above
I would care for its growth in life
And pray that among us there'd be no strife
Each locality would be at peace
In following Christ we would not cease
Each member would receive the same care
Both in love and prayer
The Lamb would be our only delight
Keeping His purpose in sight
We would all long to marry our Bridegroom
Making for Him in our hearts a comfortable room

Was there ever another man born to die
This can only be said of our Lord on high
The cross marked His life
And His creatures caused Him such strife
But He did it all
For the people of the Fall
No complaint from Him was ever heard
Of His love we are assured
Now I wonder how my Jesus can be so good
How can His tender heart be understood
It is love of a higher kind
That is only in God's heart and mind
Man this never can attain
It's solely found in the One Who was slain
So let's exalt Him alone
This exquisite Redeemer, now on His throne

It's a life built on trust and reliance
So there would be no defiance
It is not in striving much
But to have a grace touch
The Lord can do it all
We just in faith need to call
His supply is more than enough
To carry us through times that are rough
All wisdom has He
Following Jesus makes us free
But if we choose our own way
Misery will fill the day
So wisdom use
Don't because of self lose
Then Christ's smile you will see
Child of the jubilee

Remember, in my spirit is a stream
It's a living one, this is no dream
In me it does flow
Satisfaction to know
It has the sweetest taste
When I awake to go there I make haste
On Christ I start to call
I almost forget I am a man of the Fall
I must make this my daily routine
Then good results will be seen
Stronger my spirit will grow
The divine life deeper to know
Christ will abide within
And I'll conquer troublesome sin
The effort I will make
For His glory's sake

Don't take offense when the Lord does admonish
Thee it ought not to astonish
For the one that He does love
He disciplines from above
Great is His care
His holy nature He wants us to share
Sinners we are on our own
But by the blood we can approach His throne
A gentle rebuke we may hear
Don't be afraid to still draw near
Overcorrect Jesus will not
He just wants to be inwrought
He will gently persuade
So your faults will fade
So be of good cheer
For our Lord is so very near
And when His work is done
How we'll shine forth God's Son

Nature is beautiful to the eye
But it will never satisfy
Flowers and trees
Should bring you to your knees
Your Creator to praise
For His ingenious ways
Birds and bees
Cannot really please
It takes the love of the Lamb
And belief in the Great I AM
Only in this way can you be filled
And your seeking heart satisfied and stilled
For enjoyment He gives all things
But pleasure in Him, satisfaction to our Lord brings
So don't lift up Creation
Keep it in its proper station
And enjoy Christ alone
On His exalted throne

I have not learned the full meaning of rest
On my own I must not just try my best
But learn to give my life to the Lord
Living by the strength He does afford
Or else in a constant struggle I will be
Not finding the way to be free
Peace will elude
If I don't take Christ as my true food
Overcome by His supply
His ability not to deny
This is the way peace to gain
From just self-effort refrain
With my old man the Lord must deal
The effects of the cross I must feel
If crossed out am I
Then will shine my Lord on high
And attained will be His goal for me
A Christ-expressing humanity

When I witness, take my time
To properly explain salvation sublime
For I have Good News to tell
Of a Savior so loving and so swell
Forgiveness, people need to know
The seed in them I can sow
Of the Kingdom they can partake
And avoid the fiery lake
Patiently explain each main point
Let the Spirit my words anoint
That their inner man they will touch
The truth to care for much
Their conscience the Spirit would prick
To know with sin they are sick
Then for healing they would yearn
The Savior to trust and no longer spurn

I have a God Who with joy is rife
And is saturated with life
He invites me to taste and see
How good He is for me
Depression does not have to be mine
I can enjoy the Divine
In life there are disappointing things
But calling on His name comfort brings
So inwardly don't glance
Like King David, before the Lord dance
Express your love for Him
Then you'll have peace to the brim
Jesus died so that you would live
A joyful life, honor to Him does give
So let the praises start
And you'll see all sadness depart

Calling on His name
Can save from a life of sin and shame
In faith saying, "Lord Jesus," there is such power
It can rescue you each temptation hour
Exercise your spirit strong
Then victory to you will belong
Christ made the way
To walk in the light of day
Perseverance it does require
And for holiness a strong desire
Cooperation you also need
As on His faithfulness you feed
Christ your strength is He
Just approach Him on bended knee
In prayer you can make this thine
And live a life so fine

Delicious is Christ my Lord
Feasting on Him is my reward
This pleasure is so fine
It makes me want to forever dine
It's also a great pleasure to hear my King
His voice makes sense out of everything
I may not understand all
But for comfort on Him I can call
I'm so glad I have His name
My wild ways it did tame
For when we call
He forgives all
But with faith it must be united
As Scripture has cited
Remember, it's not I, but Christ my Friend
Who sin's tyranny did end!

There is always joy to be found when you drink
Deep into the Spirit you must sink
Pleasurable waters there flow
For His saints here below
Our Christ is a current so fine
Who brings in the sweet wine
Pure as crystal it surely is
Cleansing those who are His
It causes our inner man to spring
It is a most delightful thing
This river will flow for aye
With freshness every day
Lukewarm it won't be
But satisfying to you and me
A joint venture it will be
God's and man's thirst quenched entirely

Mercy, Christ wants me to show
Just as on me this He does bestow
Not as found in just my being
But as it dwells in our God unseen
Jesus displayed it all
When He rescued us from the Fall
The scourging He took
As it says in the Good Book
He even carried His own cross
Despite the strength and blood that He lost
And when they nailed His hands and feet
To the Father His work was so sweet
No condemnation did He give
He just died so that others could live
Now He's enthroned in the universe's highest place
Fully dispensing His amazing grace

Listen to the Lord before I speak
Or havoc I may wreak
Listen with an attentive ear
Speak with godly fear
Don't just offer an opinion
Let Christ have His dominion
Consult the Lord in all that I say
Before I speak surely pray
Then His wisdom will show
And the Lord's will they will know
True wisdom on my own have not I
It's Christ word that must edify
He knows the situation at hand
He alone the truth does command
So Lord, we shall follow Thee
In all You decree

O the marvels of my Friend
They will never end
Of this unlimited King
Eternal praises I can forever sing
Jesus is His name
His riches I must proclaim
The world hungers for the satisfaction that He can bring
But they seek it in every other thing
So open our mouths we must
Showing how the Savior they can trust
Explain the story slow and sure
Keeping our words true and pure
Give them an invitation to believe
By faith, eternal life to receive
Then give them a shepherd's care
Guarding them in love and prayer

What I like is not the main thing
Rather that I'd give real worship to the King
Whate're may be the worship style of others
I must remember they are my sisters and brothers
To the church we all belong
And we praise the same Christ in song
The same Holy Spirit does guide
And in the same Father we confide
So division why have
Be each other's healing salve
Differences lay aside
And in the truth abide
The Good Book we all go by
It tells of the same Savior Who for us did die
The one Body are we
Christ's glory for all to see

Let the Lord Jesus be my All in all
Don't delight in the things of the Fall
For our pleasures
Really are not treasures
A delightful way to spend the day
Is in spirit to sweetly pray
The Scripture to read
To grow the implanted seed
Fellowship with a dear brother
Satisfies like no other
Sharing the gospel with a wounded soul
Is the way to make both of you whole
Works of compassion done
For the glory of God's Son
These are the things that are true
And will please Christ Jesus and you

At times discouraged over almost nothing am I
Come to the Comforter instead of to sigh
My countenance He will lift
And I'll no longer in sorrow go adrift
I think I'm weaker than I should be
Lord, I need the great strength of Thee
For a fallen man am I
Only on Thee can I rely
Self I cannot trust
Or I'll go bust
But my King Jesus has the vigor
To live a life of rigor
I need only His supply tap
Then I'll feed on the vine's sap
This will surely carry me through
To the Jerusalem that's New

Praise makes the way
For Christ to operate in you each day
He loves the praises of His people
Wherever we may be, not just under a church steeple
It's not just the words that we speak
But our following Him week after week
The things on the inside matter to Him
Being filled with the Spirit to the brim
Our living an outflow of His life
Presenting a Christ without strife
Not a life of miracles and show
But one in which Christ we deeply know
A life that pleases our Father and God
One that does not always draw a correcting rod
So Lord, make me a good friend
One faithful to the end

For His goodness, love the Lamb
All that He is as the great I AM
A Redeemer and a King
The One of Whom all heaven does sing
A Shepherd and a Friend
The One Who with all my time I like to spend
A Beacon and the Light
The One Who never is trite
Our Lord and our God
The One Who reached down to touch this earthly sod
A Prince and a High Priest
The One Who loves the greatest to the least
So many wonderful things is He
More of Him I'd love to see
In eternity, full and clear will be our portion
For no more will sin cause distortion
Then Christ we'll know to the uttermost
Truly blessing the Lord of hosts

Coming to a place of trust in the Lord
That only experience and time can afford
Worthy of it He surely is
The One Who made this sinner His
The evidence is much
That you can trust His gentle touch
Your life He can wisely direct
As you, He did elect
Don't spend your whole life shying away
From the Lord Who in your spirit is there to stay
When He extends His love to you
Do what you must do
Take it all
Don't for another moment stall
Then pleasantly surprised you shall be
By the tender heart of the Lord of glory

My senses I must not indulge
For it has caused my midsection to bulge
For cookies and cream
My tongue might scream
But over me such must not hold power
Not for a single day or hour
Self-control at times I lack
And from making good choices I slack
But I must make prudence mine
And be wise like Christ divine
I'm sure He was fit and trim
In torso and limb
His body was a temple so fine
He would not indulge when He did dine
So my portions I will cut
And be saved from this enslaving rut

For people truly care
Always lifting them up in prayer
Then you'll be like your King
And praise to Jesus you'll bring
For souls He has great concern
His loving heart you must discern
He wants to save every living being
He's doing work by us unseen
Hearts He is preparing
As the gospel we are sharing
So undaunted be
Tell of His salvation liberally
Perhaps a fish you will catch
And Christ will make a beautiful life out of a wretch
For that was once my state
Until Christ myself did recreate
Now I can only tell of His wonder
As my soul from hell He did plunder

Lord, there is nothing better to do
Other than to truly praise You
Nothing else can lift my spirit higher
Or make me for Thee more on fire
At times I search my mind
If there is another way joy to find
But I only come up dry
Why did I even try
The answer I already knew
Joy is only found in You
I must stop my pointless ways to search
Just come to Christ and the church
The abundance there is great
Right now is not too late
So Lord, on Thee I'll forever dine
And make Your joy all mine!

Learn to trust
For salvation that is a must
But in daily life too
Rely on Jesus in all that you do
A helpful Friend is He
Carrying your load for thee
His arms are strong
And for you He suffers long
There is no better guide
In Whom you can confide
In Him your confidence place
As you run the Christian race
Then you will finish well
His praises to forever tell
And when your trust is complete
You'll truly know that Jesus is so sweet

The Lord's love I must truly know
That's the only way to trust and grow
If I think He doesn't care
And won't listen to my prayer
Then my heart won't be warm enough
And I might be a little rough
So to truth I must pay attention
Nowhere does the Bible God's fickleness mention
For His children there is no such thing
God only love and correction does bring
No wrong has He ever done
To me His precious son
So I must not listen to lies
They don't come from a Savior Who in love dies
Toward us there is only goodness immense
So no longer will my countenance be tense

Christ has promised you a hope and a future
To always give you tender nurture
Back on His word He will not go
For good seed into you He did sow
You are His blessed treasure
He bestows on you love beyond measure
The timing of things in your life
Is not meant to cause you strife
But its purpose is as high
As God above the sky
So receive it all by His grace
Every trial in Him with courage face
You they will not break
But into a godly family make
So endure for another season
And one day, the Lord will make known every reason

For all of mankind let my love be the same
For every family on earth bears the Father's name
Not everyone is a child of the King
But some expression of Christ they bring
For in His image they are made
And Christ's life down for them was laid
So Lord, increase my care
As the gospel with them I share
You would love to see peace in our land
And not to the sword to put our hand
Lord, work in each heart
The beginning of faith to start
For if all believed
The troubles of earth would be relieved
And I know when You return
We'll have the world for which we yearn

Be content with your wages
It says so on Scripture's pages
The Lord will provide
Your duty is to trust and abide
Let not the love of money be your way
But on Christ Jesus your heart would stay
Only He can fill you up
With worldliness do not sup
Let your heart's affection
Only be in Christ's direction
For He solely is worthy of adoration
This wise Author of Creation
Lord, we were made for Thee
To love and exalt this lone Deity
For until that is done
There cannot be rich enjoyment of God's Son

Don't let sin mar your vision
Of the Lord now risen
Let Christ be the cure
To keep your heart pure
To see Him clear
And into eternity to peer
You must live a life that is holy
Making Him your goal solely
For sin does fellowship break
And peace away it does take
Don't let it rule your life
Filling it with strife
Instead be like your King
Then in joy you will sing
This is the way life is meant to be
As Adam and Eve in the garden did see

Give your all to the Lord
For a bountiful reward
But for the right reasons follow Him
That your heart overflows with love to the brim
For your motives He cares
This One, Who numbers all of your hairs
Let them be pure
That for His glory you endure
You love to make much of Christ the King
And rejoice to hear others His praises sing
Remember, it's not about you and me
But that Christ only others would see
He alone deserves adulation
For He is the Author of Creation
So lift up this magnificent Son
And for Him the race faithfully run

I want to cooperate with the Lord in all things
These words such joy to Jesus brings
If I take my hands off of my life
Christ will rule without strife
He's been waiting a long time
To be in practice my Lord sublime
But I often refuse
To let Him myself sovereignly use
The commands that He has already given
In these must be my livin'
That will free the way
For even more wonderful things to hear Him say
I do want the Lord's best
So His patience I must not test
And Lord, of Thee I ask
Make me faithful to every ordered task
Then I know Your heart will be glad
For Your way will finally be had

Our joy on circumstance does not depend
It's found in the anointing of Jesus our Friend
Trials can abound
But in Him peace can be found
Foul the weather can be
But Lord, there's still sunshine in Thee
Our finances can be low
We can be assailed by the foe
But if You we know
Joy can only flow
For when Your brothers experience Thee
Doom turns to glee
No other person can do what You do
Making a sad heart bloom anew
So Lord, why did I ever pout
When I can take Thee as my joyful route

Don't look for an easy way out
The Lord's wisdom don't doubt
Trying times He may let you go through
In them just follow what He says to do
He will strengthen the saint that you are
And you'll know Jesus better by far
Keep the word that you give
That by faith you want to live
This is the way to please
Not a life of ease
His grace is more than enough
To sustain when life is rough
But it takes a believing heart
That from His way will not depart
Just rest assured that He is good
Even if all by you is not understood

The same mercies that Jesus shows me
I want to give to humanity
But especially my sisters and brothers
Not neglecting others
The grace that's in His heart
I want to learn to impart
That others would be impressed with the Lord
Touching an unheard chord
That their lives too would sing
Bringing enjoyment to the King
They His wisdom would come to know
And in their lives it would show
But they need to learn godly fear
And to Christ, in spirit draw near
Then all will be clear
And each soul will know true cheer

My Lord Jesus is amazing
His love I am forever praising
He is my sweet delight
For He's given me spiritual sight
I can see the goodness of His heart
For such grace to me He does impart
His love He gives to the extreme
Beyond my wildest dream
In eternity I will fully plumb its depth
As it takes away my breath
How we'll all be drawn to the King
Only His praises to forever sing
No longer will self be an issue
For there will be no more sin in our tissue
But pristine our souls shall be
So we can dwell in the light of His glory

Endless delight awaits those who believe
From the Lord such mercy they did receive
A dull moment there won't be
Or sins to separate you and me
Our love will be pure
No more troubles to endure
Fellowship more than fine
An endless feast on which to dine
A Savior to truly praise at last
And no more reasons to fast
The music will be O so sweet
As the Lord Jesus with songs we treat
How pleasant the surroundings will be
And how glorious them to finally see
But Jesus will be front and center
Into His presence to forever enter

Don't think I know better than my King
For He's the sovereign Creator of everything
Incomparable His wisdom is
I am a mere child of His
But my thoughts He wants to hear
And guide them to a godly fear
Then my life would be much better
And sin would not be a fetter
In this area I have grown
But more of His ways must be known
Much patience has been given
To slowly correct my livin'
His tender ways appreciate do I
As He trains me to comply
How I thank my Teacher and Lord
For all the goodness this life does afford

What I want is not the main thing
But that glory to Christ I would bring
My concern should be His will
What in me He can instill
A faithful walk
Godly actions, not much talk
A submissive attitude
And a heart of gratitude
Love for my sisters and brothers
And compassion for others
The gospel always to share
With a heart that honestly does care
These are the desires of my Lord
Accomplished by the grace He does afford
So submit to them I must
As I learn to fully trust

Be kind to others
Whether or not they are sisters or brothers
A bad day they may have
So be their healing salve
An apt word speak
As their comfort you seek
It can turn a heart around
And perhaps a new friend will be found
For our God is the Prince of Peace
And He wants striving between souls to cease
If the Savior they don't know
A good word you can sow
Root in them take it might
If Christ on them shines the light
Just be in prayer
And show that you care

About old age I need not worry
Or to get there to be in a hurry
For when there I arrive
In my Jesus I still can thrive
Hopefully a little wiser I shall be
Having experienced much more of Thee
And fruit I shall still reap
As His word I keep
My love will have grown
Christ in me being deeply sown
I hope my regrets will be few
As I've done what Jesus said to do
And as I've shared life with my wife
Our times will end with sweetness, not strife
So Lord, call us to Your side
Forever with Thee to abide

A delightful time together we had
Before I came I was feeling a little sad
But my soul you did cheer
As for fellowship we drew near
I hope some love and peace I did impart
To your friendly heart
It's good to know other believers
For we are grace receivers
This is good for building up
As we encourage each other with Christ to sup
For our friendship He cares
To keep each other in our prayers
Practical help we'd also give
For that is the Christian life to live
Together we look forward to that day
When for our love, "Well done," Christ shall say

All that we do
Should be a glory to the One Who made us born anew
For apart from Him
We would have sin to the brim
But He conquered that ugly blight
And made our sins snow white
Now righteously we can live
Praise to Christ to give
And as we glorify our King
We lift Him to the stature of a holy thing
And the pleasant Lamb
Is remembered as the Great I AM
The Father is pleased to the uttermost
As we recognize Christ, the Lord of hosts
For Jesus is the universe's center
The only way glory to enter

Learn to trust Christ's leading
For that is what you are truly needing
Let Him the Lord be
Don't encroach on His territory
He is God alone
The only one with a sovereign throne
No mistake will He ever make
He'll rightly guide you for your sake
All wisdom to Him belongs
And no one He ever wrongs
So compliant be
Acknowledging His loving authority
Against Him don't be proud
Of rebellion that speaks loud
The sooner Him you follow
Quicker will be gone times that are hollow
Then joy will fill your days
Calling for unending praise

How blessed am I to have my Lord
No better riches could any other afford
No greater love could there be
Than that of the Trinity
Each has been so good to me
Their loveliness I can see
Jesus in His passion died
Now in Him I confide
He lets me tell Him each heartache of mine
Then He gives comfort divine
The Father I better need to know
And closer to Him grow
The Spirit I love to drink
To Christ He is my link
More than blessed am I
Fully graced by God on high

Hold no grudges at all within
For unforgiveness is a sin
The Lord forgave it all
So my heart cannot be small
With me He has peace
So others I must fully release
It's not my prerogative to stew
Over what others do
I must still be kind
If an offense I find
When I consider how I've hurt my Lord
Bitterness I cannot afford
I must be gentle and sweet
To all souls that I meet
Then greatly glorified will be Christ the King
And I may even hear heaven sing

That dear wife of mine
She's a gift from the Lord divine
She's precious to my soul
To complete and make me whole
She's my better half as they say
Sweeter becoming day be day
With a love that is tender
Growing, as to Christ she does surrender
There's much about her that I don't know
So closer we must grow
I love how she cares for my family and friends
And kindness and well wishes she sends
In the church she serves
And I believe a good reward she deserves
But my greatest desire
Is that for Jesus she'd more on fire

God's wrath I would not want to face
I thank Jesus for His saving grace
I'm so glad I was chosen by the Lamb
To spend eternity with the Great I AM
No longer under God's displeasure
Now to Him I am a little treasure
Kindness to me He does speak
No more with evil do I wreak
How the Lord wants to be with me
Keeping sweet company
All this, because faith to me was given
Bringing me through the veil now riven
There I have such delight with my King
Loud hallelujahs I love to sing
To think that for all eternity this will last
Because my sins into the deepest sea were cast

How glad am I for Your precious blood divine
That makes me all Thine
I was headed for a dreadful pit
That with fire was lit
But by Your sovereign decree
You had such mercy on me
Now rescued am I
So that to Jesus I can draw nigh
Such tender words I hear
Quenching all of my fear
But respect my Lord I must
And give Him all my trust
He is a faithful, loving Friend
But His will does not bend
So Lord, I want to lead a godly life
Not creating between us any strife
Then we two shall have delight
Because by grace, I followed what was right

It's by His tender grace that I love my wife
Or else my heart would know only strife
Marriage is good
When Christ's ways are understood
Compassion we can show
As Jesus we come to know
Forbearance is not foreign to Irena and me
For in our Lord, it we abundantly see
To each other we relinquish our rights
Thereby avoiding needless fights
Seeds of discord are not sown
As we obey our Lord on His throne
Pleasant and comfortable we are with each other
For in Christ we are sister and brother
How I thank the Lord for a marriage that is fine
As together, on Jesus we dine

For our friendship I care
As I keep you in my prayer
Times together are sweet
My life you help to complete
It seems by chance we met
But with Christ it was a sure bet
Better we've come to know each other
Brother with brother
We support each other with love
As Jesus watches over us from above
He is pleased we show compassion
That is not always found in this world's fashion
Often we talk on the phone
Our friendship to hone
In eternity we'll have much time
To fellowship together with Christ sublime

Christ grows me each day
As I listen and obey
He's my strength year by year
As I live in godly fear
His blessings He pours out
His goodness I must never doubt
Precious is His every thought to me
My growth He does guarantee
For one day I'll be just like Him
With love and joy to the brim
Our God, He works in mysterious ways
For He's the all-knowing Ancient of Days
When with Christ I stand face to face
I long for a sweet embrace
So proper I shall live
Then perhaps a "Well done" He will give

To really live
Is to others to give
For self we were not made
Rather glory to Christ would be paid
Him we would exalt at every turn
For fellowship with Him to yearn
Only this makes sense
To live for Him hence
We would love Him with our whole being
For that is truly freeing
Inward we would not look
But upward to the Christ of the Good Book
Satisfy us that shall
And all will be well
For the secret we now know
Live Christ in the flow

I've been reconciled
No longer constantly defiled
The Triune God became my Friend
My old life He did end
Now my desires are holy and new
For I'm born anew
With that comes privileges and rights
And comfort in the dark nights
Death no longer to fear
Christ now to me is very dear
Him I'll be able to face
As I live by grace
On bedrock my life I must build
As with the Spirit I am filled
No longer living in vain
But my Christ to love and gain
Then when life is through
My regrets will be few

What a blessing You are to me
King Jesus, the Lord of glory
When You find me down
Of Your lovely voice I hear the sound
Uplift me it will
To my heart it is a thrill
When a great burden I feel
You remind me You're at the wheel
My life You direct
For the best effect
When loneliness comes upon me
I have sweet fellowship with Thee
To me that time is so dear
How I love to have You near
How glad am I that I met Thee
And I'll be with You eternally

Lord, I went astray in sin
But You brought back this lamb once again
I had only known death
With every breath
By the Good Shepherd I was sought
And with the Triune God I was inwrought
This blessing is almost too much
To have the Savior's gentle touch
How could there be such mercy
Bestowed on one so lost and thirsty
Now in my life it is a fact
This excellent salvation act
My life cannot better be
Except at last, when Jesus I see
Awaits such love and affection
How thankful am I for my election

Listen to the Lamb
For He is the great I AM
He's sovereign over you
So do all He says to do
Do it without a murmur or complaint
For you are a blood bought saint
It should be your duty and delight
With Christ don't put up a fight
To do His will you should be glad
For mercy on you He has had
He doesn't really ask that much
Just permit Him your will to tenderly touch
Love Him with every part
Of your God-renewed heart
Then Christ and His Body will have peace
As your hold on life you release

Jesus is my song
As He is all the day long
How I love to sing His praise
What a wonderful way to spend my days
When songs fill my heart
A bad mood won't even start
From turmoil I am free
Christ's heart to more clearly see
I can perceive His love
As I make melody to my Lord God above
It even refreshes my King
To hear me pleasantly sing
I'm so glad music He did create
Such a beautiful way our love to state
It makes our feelings easy to show
And causes our spirits strong to grow
What an incredible gift
Our voices evermore, Him to uplift

I was falling into despair
Then I met a Savior Who did care
In person He came down
And by His love I was found
Into His arms He welcomed me
There was a glint in His eyes I could see
I knew the fight was through
When I was born anew
That was the best experience in my life
When with the Triune God there was no more strife
A reconciliation was made
For my pardon by Christ was paid
Now is the time to grow
And like Christ be meek and low
The divine life I can savor
For with my God I've found favor
All the glory to Christ does go
For apart from Him, forgiveness I would never know

Care for one another in truth and deed
Lovingly meeting each believer's need
Christ did many loving acts
These are simply the facts
Out of His way He always went
For this purpose He was sent
He always lent a hand
Obeying His Father's every command
The same we should do
If we love Christ and people too
How self gets in the way
For strength we must trust and pray
Our intentions might be good
But we're still sinners is understood
So look to Jesus for grace
Then you'll bless the human race

I come to the Lamb Who took away my sin
Never to have to hide from Him again
Reconciled and adored
No wrath for me is stored
Pleasant times await
From the One Who me did create
Why should I have such blessings and love
From this holy God above
It's because of the kindness of His heart
And the faith that Christ did impart
Or else what would the Lord with me have to do
For I was a sinner through and through
But by His grace
He redeemed me, a member of the fallen race
Now happy am I
For the second death I will not die

O to comply
Christ's will never to deny
That would be true bliss
Disobedience my Lord would not miss
As He hears me say yes
How Christ it does bless
His heart is greatly gladdened
And no longer am I saddened
There seems to be dysfunction in me
For I don't do all I hear or see
Procrastinate often do I
In a way, this His will does deny
Or the fear that I display
Causes me to go my own way
Jesus Lord save
This is not the way I want to behave

It's all of grace
The way to run this race
No ability have I
My Lord Jesus to satisfy
Rely on Him is all I can do
This soul now born anew
Before I believed
No instruction had I ever received
Now I have the Lord's direction
I must follow with much affection
I can't cling to my own ways
I was made Him to trust and praise
Like the angels holy
I must glorify Him solely
And I know my Savior will do it all
If I just listen to His call

I must keep my word to Thee
Not defiling my humanity
To be like You
I must say things true
Never back on Your promises went Thee
But kept them so faithfully
Sometimes a challenge it I find
To do so in kind
For a sinful nature have I
Regrettably, I don't always comply
I know You forgive
But Lord Jesus, that's not how I want to live
Sometimes it is just fear
Or I hold my own will too dear
Overcome by faith can I
My sins to defy
Then happy will be my King
And I know I'll hear Him joyfully sing

"Wise men still seek Him," that
card you sent me long ago
More of this truth I'm coming to know
It's been a good ride
This fact cannot be denied
I hope you also find this true
In your faith and daily life too
How I pray the Lord Jesus to bless thee
With love, hope, and longevity
That with your family, contentment you'd find
But also knowing what's on Christ's mind
For He is your life
The One Who saves you from pressure and strife
He says make Me your goal alone
And enjoy Me at My gracious throne
Then real purpose will be yours
This the Holy Word assures

Seek ye the Lord while He may be found
And you He shall surely astound
The depth of His wisdom and love
Is as high as the heavens above
A lover at heart is He
Forgiving so willingly
A King to be sought above all
A name to forever enjoy and call
A blessedness that cannot be understood
And a question: how can You be so good
When my sins I consider
I wonder why the Lord is not bitter
But I'm forgiven because of grace
And I see a smile on Jesus' face
So happy I must be
For Jesus is my jubilee

My only joy is the Lamb
How sweet to be touched by the Great I AM
In your spiritual senses you can tell
The Savior for you does all things well
He is much more than a Friend
He to your every need does attend
He constantly watches over you
And guides in all that you must do
He is almost too kind
How such treasure did we find
Just to think, At one time we were blind
Not even having Christ on our mind
But when He took the blinders away
What wonderful words did He say
O child, My beloved you are
And I am your bright Morning Star
So for My return watch and wait
For I am soon coming and won't be late

Be at peace with others
For they are your precious sisters and brothers
How Jesus wants you to be one
For you are joined together in the Son
Unspeakable joy this gives
To the One Who in us all lives
His heart has great delight
With His brothers at peace, never to fight
For gentle are the Lord's ways
We being the same gives Him sweet praise
So at our differences look past
To say I'm sorry be fast
We will glorify Christ even more
If the best in others we adore
And remember, only human are we
So weak in our humanity

Drink Jesus so sweetly
Enjoy Him completely
Your portion could never be better
For He is Alpha and Omega and every other letter
Never tired of dining are we
Enjoying Him in simplicity
Never harden we our heart
Keeping our countenance sweet, not tart
Faithful I always want to be
According to His estimate of me
We know sin He does not condone
But the forgiven can always approach His throne
There they will find a tender time
Fellowshipping with the sublime
So in your wisdom be astute
For Christ always bearing fruit
Then all that will remain
Is the Christ that we did gain

Don't worry about what lies ahead
For our Savior is raised from the dead
He has all might
And for you He shall fight
If overwhelmed you're feeling
A look at Him will give healing
He cares about your frame of mind
Peace in it He longs to find
But you need to look away
To the Christ to Whom you pray
He can rescue from distress
And give your soul a gentle caress
He says, Come away and be with Me
For I am your comfort and security
No other Savior do you need
For I am the only One Who can faithfully lead

All people learn to better love
That's a divine principle from above
Jesus puts it into my heart
From selfishness I must depart
Serve my fellowman
As God did plan
My own good neither seek alone
But that I'd manifest the grace of His throne
Christ for His comfort did not care
Our burdens He so lovingly did bear
He manifested His Father's goodness
With mercy and no rudeness
He loved others to bless
As their hurts He daily did address
Worship this King we surely must
As we put in Him all of our trust

Let the Lord do the work
But at the same time, my responsibility do not shirk
For it is God Who does the working and willing
As truth and grace into us He is instilling
No credit can I take
For He is the One Who saves from the fiery lake
Gladly, abundant is His mercy
Always watering the seeking thirsty
He made my salvation sweet
In Christ He accomplished this feat
All to the Lamb I now owe
Who made my sins as white as snow
How praiseworthy is Christ the Light
From morning until night
So Lord, consume all my days
By living in Your ways
Then how glad Your heart will be
And the same will be said of me

How the Lord cares about us in trials
He'd like to always give us smiles
But shallow would be our soul
So He lets tribulations take their toll
His heart does weep
When in distress we lose sleep
But to comfort He is there
Always with His tender care
For He is a gentle Lamb
But with the strength of I AM
It pleases Him so
That we'd trust Him as we grow
He never wants to hurt or harm
So at trials have no alarm
He will cause every pain
To be a perfect way that Christ we would gain
So complain not shall I
Or my good Savior ever deny

In Christ I am forgiven
In Him I am truly livin'
There is no greater treasure
Than to find in Him my pleasure
The new lease He gave me on life
Vanquished my ugly strife
Malice was replaced with love
To reflect the good of Christ above
From self I turned to others
To bless my sisters and brothers
From hoarding for my own
To support the work of God's throne
From things that were vain
To helping ease my neighbor's pain
It is all the work of my Lord
That the greatness of His heart does afford

Live before the Lord
A life that deserves a reward
Don't squander even one hour
Let Christ your living empower
Your actions can give praise
To Jesus for all of your days
Jesus can be glorified in you
If on your promises you follow through
He doesn't take your words lightly
Idle speaking is unsightly
So your words carefully weigh
Will they give grace today
And if they do
Jesus will be happy with you
So pleasing to Him continue to be
Then His kindness you will see

My Lord watches over me
So why should I worried be
He knows my heart's every care
He says over them have some prayer
If I bring them to His throne
Worries I will no longer own
My Lord Jesus will take away every fret
With His power it is a sure bet
He'll comfort me with His tender love
Raining down peace from above
This sweet Savior I should not doubt
For He knows me inside out
He knows just what I need
This God Who for me did bleed
So I will put my worries to rest
For in Christ I am surely blessed

Ashamed of the gospel don't be
For it is the power of God to you and me
It sets the captives free
To enjoy Christ's liberty
It gives the homeless a home
No more in the desert to roam
It brings in the Fountain of Life
For with joy it is rife
It brings peace to the troubled heart
And for Christ sets them apart
It lifts your countenance up
When with Jesus you sup
Any problem it can undo
If you've been born anew
Praise the Lord for such a word
A sweeter sound has never been heard

The Lord has total control
And He watches over my wife's soul
She's in His tender care
As I keep her in prayer
A single hair cannot perish
Of this lady whom I cherish
For she belongs to Him
Spirit, soul, and limb
Even though her I adore
He loves her so much more
His beloved is she
In all her humanity
I know she loves our Lord
And for her service, she'll have a reward
Together growing are we
Giving each other liberty
Someday soon we'll be with Jesus our Friend
Our life's perfect end

Don't doubt what the Lord for me does feel
His love and kindness is surely real
He displays it every day
By the good He does and the things I hear Him say
There is really no room for doubt
As this love He carries out
How deep it is
Is only known by those who are His
More it could never be
For it is already infinity
It blazes in His heart
Daily this love to impart
How it gladdens
What the world only saddens
It is a beacon of hope divine
This precious love of Christ's design

Our Jesus is delightful
And so insightful
He knows the reasons for our ways
And the authenticity of our praise
Are we truly motivated by love
To magnify our Lord above
Do we seek applause
And notice a brother's little flaws
Or are we tender and kind
Having the Lord's mind
Let our Christ get the glory
And be busy telling His story
Then how much richer life will be
And true joy you will see
Let your life be about Him
Then you'll know satisfaction to the brim

For righteousness hunger and thirst
Always keeping Christ first
Don't serve Him halfway
All laziness slay
For He surely deserves your all
If you're one who upon His name does call
For He has given His best
Now your love He will test
If you want to succeed
With Him in view, do every good deed
But make sure it is one He did ordain
From self-glory refrain
Then Jesus you shall gain
As you exalt the Lamb once slain
Leave no command of His undone
Then you'll have the exceeding joy of God's Son

I have reason to rejoice
I hear my Savior's voice
A loving rebuke He may give
It's only so that by His life I may live
An encouraging word
Is almost daily heard
Never does He demean
His caring ways are always seen
He provides the best spiritual care
As I engage Christ in prayer
On Him I can cast every anxious thought
And His wise counsel can always be sought
A song He always gives me to sing
A cheerful heart it faithfully does bring
I guess you can call me blessed
But Jesus just loves me like all the rest

Don't eye the things that we own
Soon they'll be idols of wood and stone
Lifeless are they
They'll never answer when you pray
But our God is alive
In Jesus, His love does thrive
Only He can fill that inner void
All else will only leave you annoyed
Our God to us shall forever speak
To carry out His will, never is He weak
The one perfect Sacrifice was He
Now to Him we come on bended knee
Our requests He will hear
Especially when we ask Him to draw near
And with His perfect love
He showers down affection from above

Don't turn away
Always listen to what Christ has to say
He has wisdom to share
To show you how to truly care
On your own you have not the strength
To follow Him for all your life's length
So learn to be humble
Over pride do not stumble
Admit your need
That you require His lead
Time will surely tell
The unbelieving were the ones who fell
So your faith let Him grow
As more of Christ and His Word you come to know
Then your end will be fine
As you do all that He does assign

Lord Jesus, I have nothing but praise for Thee
For all of eternity
So worthy Thou art
Kind words from my mouth shall never depart
Laud Thee I truly must
Even more so, as Thee I learn to fully trust
In my heart are the issues of life
Toward Thee I must never have any strife
You are good to me every day
Hallelujah, I must surely say
When You come to carry me home
I'll be glad that from Thee, no longer shall I roam
I know my place in Thee is secure
For Thy truth shall forever endure
And now contentment I am learning
As for Thee alone I am yearning

Saint, when you're feeling dry
Come to the Lord Jesus for His supply
His waters never fail
And will brighten your countenance once pale
Your heart they will cheer
Maybe you'll cry a joyful tear
Gone will be any lingering sadness
Praise the Lord for His gladness
It's only by His life divine
That again you're feeling fine
How much thanks we ought to give
For the privilege in Him to live
Although it's available to all
Not everyone upon Him will call
Never believe the lie
That life is just one long sigh
For in the Lord we can always rejoice
If we listen to His voice

Hail His return
For Jesus alone should we yearn
Only He can fill us up
So with the Lamb faithfully sup
You can sing or shout
Just don't lock Him out
Keep your heart open and free
Commune with Him on bended knee
He will hear your prayer
Remember how much He does care
If you forget, just gaze at the cross
And at the life with which He paid our cost
It was a life pure and sweet
Redemption's requirements to meet
No one else could carry this work out
But our King did it, so hallelujah shout

When He finally transforms and
transfigures His believers
We'll be of joy the greatest receivers
When that eternal age does begin
How we'll rejoice that there is no more sin
Obedience will be complete
No more flesh, us to defeat
The presence of our glorious Lord
Might almost be more than our senses can afford
In Him we shall revel for aye
At all the words we hear Him say
Of the Trinity
We'll have unbounded affinity
For the trappings of the new earth
We'll forever praise Jesus for our new birth
We shall forever wonder how this could be
This incredible love for you and me!

Jesus is as warm as warm can be
And He's so tender toward you and me
From selfishness He is free
He's incredible as all believers can see
Never did He care for base gain
From the love of anything not holy, He did refrain
His thoughts were always precious and sweet
The Father's will always to meet
How He bore the thought of dying
Without for Himself crying
Is the most amazing feat of all
For us it would surely appall
But merely human not is our Lord
He has all the attributes His deity does afford
So as God the good
Perhaps His humble greatness can be understood

My time does not belong to me
It's to follow Christ as He does see
For all things to Him are known
And He wisely rules over me from His throne
So Him I must trust to run my life
Otherwise I will know only death and strife
The decisions that He does make
Are made in love for my sake
And the glory He will receive
If Him I follow, as in His goodness I believe
Sadness I often feel
I need for my Jesus to have more zeal
My will must truly bend
And Christ no longer offend
So Lord, please work this all out
And your love let me never again doubt

The Lord will give me all the grace I need
To serve Him in every good deed
To draw from self I need not do
For I have a Source since being born anew
Jesus is His name
His divine supply I can claim
So I need not fail
Nor have my life be a bitter tale
I can turn to Him
And be filled with joy to the brim
Then empowered I shall be
Doing His will with glee
Then people may take note
That I am not living by rote
But by the King of kings
Who salvation to this world brings

Obedience begets obedience
In our experience
The more we obey
The more wonderful things Christ will say
This is the pathway to true love
For our sovereign Jesus above
To our hearts He will become dearer
And to Him we'll naturally draw nearer
Our conscience will be at peace
And our frustration will cease
We'll have many more pleasant days
And we'll know the secret of His praise
Triumphant we shall be in our Lord
For this, submission does afford
So we'll stay faithful to our King
Then in delight, over us He'll sing

Ring in the New Year
With godly fear
Make this a year Jesus to gain
From all complaining refrain
Learn to rejoice every day
As homage to Christ you pay
Let His reward be an incentive to you
To do what He says to do
But let your motive be love
As you please your Savior above
Don't let life get you down
For joy in the Lord can always be found
Make this a year Jesus to trust
As unbelief your God does bust
Then when this New Year comes to an end
To the Lord Jesus you will be a better friend

Jesus will never leave you the same
When you believe into His name
Transformed your soul will be
Made like His humanity
Gone will be every rough edge
And with the truth you will not hedge
Much kinder will be your deeds
And into others you'll plant gospel seeds
Your thoughts will become holy
And your praise will be for Christ solely
Your love will grow
And the Lord you'll long to know
Your spirit will grow stronger
And you'll be willing to suffer longer
You'll look forward to being completed
Never again by sin to be defeated

Christ spoke into my life
When He blessed me with a loving wife
How I praise Him for her
I pray her kindness will tenderly endure
Now that we are joined together
As one flesh the storms of life we will weather
If I'm feeling down
Comfort in her voice is found
For she has godly cheer
This makes me want to be near
At times we may have a little miff
But Christ sees to it that there is no permanent rift
To us His grace is much
So we give each other a gentle touch
How pleased with marriage am I
With a thankful heart to Christ I cry
Together we shall pursue our dear Lord
Each hoping for a heavenly reward

My soul's desire is the Lord
And the delight that His riches do afford
These are more than enough
To carry me when life is rough
And when life takes on an easier tone
I still rejoice at Christ's throne
Everything that He does for me
Is all because of Calvary
I'm so glad He chose me to be His friend
To love and enjoy my Savior to the end
Now that I am reconciled
I guard my temple, not to be defiled
He has called me to a living that is pure
Showing kindness that will endure
Whether stranger or friend
A helpful hand I must lend
And for the gospel always care
The Good News to passionately share

I matter to Him
He's filled with loving concern to the brim
He won't let me out of His sight
Me, He always treats right
He directs each step of my life
Turning me away from all strife
He bids me Him to better know
Always wanting me to grow
He gives sweet Christians to meet
My life to complete
I have a wife better than I deserve
Lovingkindness to me she does serve
All of this I obtained for free
Even the privilege of my Savior to see
It was faith that brought me this grace
A spiritual descendent of Abraham's race

Take all things in stride
In Christ Jesus abide
He will calm your restless mind
Sweet peace in Him you'll find
The pressures of this life
Can create havoc and strife
But the wise believer
Is always a grace receiver
He knows how to tap into the Lord's supply
And to self to die
He drinks of the Lord's cup
Moment by moment with Jesus to sup
Stress overcomes him not
Living by faith is his lot
And his life is to love the Lord
With all his brothers as faith does afford

Enjoy the vine life
It's sweet without strife
It comes from the pleasant One
God's most satisfying Son
His brothers He feeds
Blessing them with good deeds
The greatest was showing love
Being God incarnate from above
He took on flesh to die
Salvation for us He did not deny
To His will how can I say no
For I want my love for Him to grow
Now that to my Beloved I belong
I want Jesus to be the reason for every song
He must have a hold on my heart
Controlling every part
Then growth will be assured
And one day I'll be matured

The Spirit too is sweet
He is God complete
He cherishes us like the Son
So much by Him is done
The Scripture is His thought
Christ's will by Him we are taught
He makes Jesus real
His tenderness your heart can feel
He is grieved when we sin
When you repent, He's at home again
He glorified Christ our Friend
Time with us He wants to spend
He's creative and kind
Infinite is His mind
And because in us He does reside
Him we must love and take His side

It's hard to take it in
That God would die for my sin
I caused Him so much pain
In me, what did the Lord gain
He thought it worthwhile
The cross' unbelievable trial
Now He has brothers filled with love
Forever praising our Savior above
He has a Body that for Him cares
And offers up precious prayers
Jesus never makes a mistake
He the best path did take
Now our hearts are filled with light
And we can choose what is good and right
That is to eat the Life Tree
With our Christ for all eternity

Don't live for selfish pleasure
I must learn my Lord's will to treasure
My life is not mine to claim
Since I've called on Jesus' name
He orders each step of my path
For He's the One Who saved me from God's wrath
Proud I must not be
Thinking I don't have to listen to Thee
Rather thanksgiving
Must permeate my living
If not for Thy grace
How could the Judge I ever face
Mercy is what I need
In always following the Savior's lead
Lord, thank You for this wake up call
Now be my All in all

The Word my thinking corrects
About the people God elects
It's not up to me to say
For others I just must pray
I know my Lord is kind
In my life this I find
Some of His ways are past finding out
But His love I must not doubt
He does nothing wrong at all
Toward people who on Him will not call
Free will given are we
But not all want to place their trust in Thee
I'm just so grateful that I belong to You
And to me You are faithful and true
Other souls I must commit to love
And tell them of my dear Savior above

My Redeemer has loved me
With the greatest that love can be
He has seen to it
That in the heavenlies with Him I sit
Companionship He sweetly does give
So with Him I will faithfully live
His kindness He does show
The more to cause me to grow
When my face has a sad expression
Unbelief is my confession
But His speaking buoys me up
So in faith with Him again I sup
Then joy is restored
As in His shelter I am moored
Over me He almost does fawn
From the break of dawn
For our Lord Jesus is more affectionate than we know
For we to Him are like a sweet doe

The weather is not under my control
Nor totally is the transformation of my soul
But with Christ I can side
And by faith in Him abide
My disposition He will change
Over its entire range
Someday, gone will be every bad mood
Never again will I be careless or rude
Peace will permeate my entire being
And faith someday will be seen
When I look into my Savior's eyes
Then I will finally know that me He does prize
Now I live with much that is unknown
But by faith I know that the Lord rules from His throne
And He is bringing this age to an end
Before it is too late dear soul,
embrace Him as your Friend

When you're feeling forlorn
Remember, Christ will never forsake you, He has sworn
His love for you away can never be torn
For into His family you were reborn
Now that you are God's child
With unbelief don't be defiled
Believe all His Word has to say
And be confident when you pray
For faith reward does He
If it's done in love you see
Each believer He wants to bless
Don't be ashamed His name to confess
It is the Lord Who us does carry
And He chose the precious ones to marry
So let's prepare for that day
And make it splendid all the way

A word spoken in due season
How good it is beyond reason
When the Lord comforts you with His speaking
Your good and love He is seeking
He gives you the best care
Far beyond your prayer
Thankful to the uttermost
Must be your heart toward the Lord of hosts
Gratitude unbounded
With lovely praise sounded
This must be your concern
As for more of Christ you yearn
For all that He has done
He deserves worship from every soul under the sun
So enlighten some woman or man
With the truth and beauty of God's good plan

Slow down, praise, and pray
Then you'll hear Jesus better day by day
His will you don't want to miss
Doing it will give you true bliss
Faint-hearted don't be
Pursue Jesus passionately
His every command keep
Even if you must lose sleep
His hallelujahs keep singing
For joy to Him that is bringing
Don't let your battle shield down
And rejoice in Jesus; don't frown
On His name always call
How that saves you from the Fall
So you see there is plenty to do
To keep you faithful and true

My Lord's heart with love is bursting
For more of me He is thirsting
Of my heart He wants all
And every morning, in love on Him I would call
I would finally let Him order my day
Taking all matters to Him as I pray
Decisions would be made in His light
His will not to fight
Then how happy Jesus would be
No longer in a struggle with me
I'm glad that patient is my good Friend
My ear to Him I shall lend
I'll let Him have control over my will
Keeping my heart before Him quiet and still
His joy promises me strength
To travel this road of any length
So Lord, overcome any unbelief in me
For You know that my heart I want to give to Thee

Christ is glad to have mercy on me
Such liberation in Him I see
A grudge never to hold
On me He is sold
How gracious is my Lord
This is surely told in His Word
And never ending it is
To those named as His
Company with us He shall always keep
Even at night during sleep
And to awake with Him on my mind
Such comfort I find
As I make my way throughout the day
I need to make sweet times to pray
For the more I contact my Friend
The more grace He will send
Such riches have we
All because of Christ, our Surety

Praise He does give
When Jesus I do live
If I reflect His grace
I see a smile on His face
For good to the world is He
Like Him I long to be
Step by step Him I gain
And from sin, by grace refrain
As truth is sought
A good fight is fought
But mingled with love it must be
For how Christ cares for humanity
His glory He put aside
And how His love and patience was tried
But He showed not one fault
The Father to exalt
His heart cried out for us to believe
All His goodness to receive
Now many have done so
The Good Shepherd to love and know

Lord Jesus, since you came into my heart
A love revolution You did start
Both friend and foe
I would love so
You are the source
That lets me walk that course
No ability have I
To love like my Lord on high
But transform my heart you do
By a supply fresh and new
I long to show that grace
To the whole human race
For that would glorify Thee
And satisfy me
So Lord, let the love begin
For in that, there is no sin

Wonderful words He spoke
And the love of many they did evoke
The love in His eyes
Showed that man He did prize
The sooner this I realize
The more I'll see the way Jesus' heart cries
The deep love of His heart
Caused Him His heavenly home to depart
On this earth He was despised and hurt
Owning not much more than His shirt
Things were not His life
But to end between God and man all strife
The cross was the only way
God's wrath toward man to stay
But our Lord died and rose
Now this truth in man He sows
And when it takes root in a soul
At last, lost man is found whole

Inside of the Lord's heart
Is a desire for each soul from sin to depart
For man He has feelings tender
To invite each one to surrender
For He knows that He is the only way joyful you can be
And the only source for true liberty
For man is in bondage to sin
Committing it again and again
But Christ is the escape route
The only One, no doubt
The way is easy that leads to life eternal
And saves from the infernal
It's as simple as trust and call
To know the One Who is All in all
Then life's meaning will be clear
To worship Christ in love and godly fear

Love each your fellowman
For Christ wants to include them in His plan
For every soul His blood was shed
To become their living Head
For outward appearance is not His concern
But their spiritual condition they would discern
It's done by the Spirit's enlightening
This is sober, but not frightening
Your sins He will show
So repentance you would know
For a Redeemer you'd see your need
That this God-man for you did bleed
Then you would have the desire to call
On the One whose name is All in all
Eternal life you then enter
Making Jesus your beloved center

Learn to love
Says my Savior Christ above
It's not about me
But how I serve others and Thee
My own interests must not occupy my mind
But consider how I'd treat others kind
For that's just what my Jesus did
With hardly much being said
He did the good in His heart
From Creation's very start
He continues it to this day
In a most wonderful way
To follow in His steps takes grace
On your own you can't keep pace
Just settle down for the ride
As in Christ you learn to abide

At times I'm unhappy with my life
By lack of faith I invite unneeded strife
Learn to look away to Him
Then my day will be bright, not dim
For Jesus has full joy and peace
Into my life, this He longs to release
But if my faith I don't exert
I'll remain feeling hurt
Angst overcomes me
And I feel self-pity
This need not be the case
If I run to the throne of grace
The supply is abundant and free
And is available whate're your need may be

The purpose of my life
Is not to live in strife
But to learn every care
With Jesus to share
I know He will bless my day
With the kind words He always does say
A heavy burden I need not feel
For any hurt or sorrow He can heal
If I cry out to my Friend
He the malaise will end
True joy I will know once again
And be glad forgiven is every sin
All my family I want the Lord to know
My hope is that to His throne they would go
So I will patiently pray
They will come to salvation someday

Christ is my true need
My joy is on Him to ever feed
He's the One of matchless worth
The only One Who could give new birth
I contemplate His mercy everyday
And I am glad it will never go away
I can praise Him for many things
But the greatest is that love and forgiveness He brings
It is almost a shock
That God is my everlasting Rock
Man's kingdom will fail
But nothing my Lord's Kingdom can assail
For eternal is His dominion
That is Bible, not opinion
When He saves the final soul
Then a new age will roll

Speak often to my King
Such inner joy this does bring
To hear Him speak a comforting word
Leaves my heart peaceful and reassured
He is the only source
That can plan my course
On my own I would fail
My wisdom next to His is truly pale
But His counsel He freely gives
And by prudence He always lives
I know help is only a call away
My Savior will often say
Cry out and give a shout that rings
For salvation this always brings
And to Jesus keep your heart turned
Then the great lesson will be learned

Jesus took away my sin
How can I live in it again
Evil I must eschew
Just as I'd run from the flu
Don't entertain an awful thought
For with a high price I was bought
Jesus calls me His own
So a holy living in Him I must hone
Sin must not master me at all
I must learn on Jesus to immediately call
Then I will be rescued with His strength
To fight sin at any length
How sweet peace is
When you follow ways that are His
This admonition I'll take as mine
A good gift from the divine

Praiseworthy is Jesus the Lamb
The most notable Great I AM
He is clothed in brilliant light
This good God Who always is right
But condemn you never shall He
If faith you have you see
For the wrath of God is no more
If Christ to you is the door
Pasture you can find
Along with peace of mind
There are living streams from which to draw
And the giving of life, no more under the law
For we are washed in blood by His grace
Our God we can now face
And I can see His countenance shine
On the saints who have the nature divine

I know I've been redeemed by the Lamb
And in me lives the Great I AM
To my spiritual senses He is real
For I have the Spirit's seal
Games He does not play
But means all that He does say
His Word is my foremost source
To keep me on course
It guides me day by day
And gives me the resources for what to pray
The enemy sends in doubt
But Jesus has the clout
In Him safe am I
As to my Savior I draw nigh
So Lord, I'm jubilant that I belong to You
And so thankful for all that You do

Lord, You've been so good to me
You are my faithful loving Daddy
You chose me from a sea of humanity
To call me away from my vanity
You make my life worthwhile
And put on my face a genuine smile
You blessed me with knowing Your Son
And appreciating all Christ has done
For if not for Him
I'd experience wrath to the brim
But He turned it all away
When yes to Jesus I did say
Now I spend my time
Getting to know Jesus sublime
This was the best decision I ever made
How can this loving act ever be repaid

Jesus gave His all
So that on Him I could call
Now I must do the same
Serving in His name
He will light my road
And carry my load
I must keep a turned heart
And from all unbelief depart
For it is faith that causes Him to move
This the Bible surely does prove
Responsibility I must not neglect
Or this my reward will affect
For maximum joy want I
So His will never deny
Then happy will be my King
And I too shall sing

My assurance comes from the Word
That I belong to the Lord
The Bible is a good Book
Where for the truth I can look
On it I can most assuredly rely
The facts you cannot deny
It says if you believe
New life you receive
I attest to this fact
That upon faith I did act
Gently my King came in to dwell
This I know full well
No one can take Jesus away
Over this I need not pray
For I've been sealed for aye
Forgiven all the way

Forbearing is our God
He does not want to use a correcting rod
He will gently chide
So by His will you would abide
He is a very patient Lord
Being as tender as He can afford
Rebuke harshly He will not
For kindness is His lot
To anger He is slow
His desire is for you to grow
In Christ He will teach
So His goal you can reach
He will make His economy clear
That to you He longs to be near
So to Him open your heart wide
And be found on His side

Rest assured, Jesus is fine
And I can claim Him as mine
For He became my sovereign Friend
Years ago when my rebellion did end
My priorities did change
As my life Christ did rearrange
Now every Lord's Day
We assemble to worship and pray
This is the highlight of my week
When Thee, with others, I seek
It's a time to feast and dine
And enjoy love so fine
With my sisters and brothers, for our Savior we care
And the Good Word we share
A little more enlightened we leave
And lots of love Jesus does receive
Only in eternity will it be better
When broken will be the last fetter

How my Father God cares
His love, like Jesus, He gladly shares
He wants all of my love
Since I've been born from above
Jesus I'm coming to know
But closer to Abba I must grow
Like I spend time with my King
My Father's praises I too must sing
He is good just like His wonderful Son
For the Two are One
All that you see in the Savior
The Father has the same holy and sweet behavior
At the Father unbelievers may rant
But to see His love it seems they can't
But "God is love" is true
It was all seen when Christ we slew

With my life I ought to praise the Lamb
For what I do gives the highest praise gives to I AM
Words are fine
But they are not always a sure sign
That my heart is true
Is more exhibited by what I lovingly do
So Lord, I want to limit my speaking
And Thee more deeply be seeking
Glory I want to more fully give
By the life I live
So Lord, shore me up
As for strength I drink Thy cup
For meager is my own power
I need to come to Thee every hour
Then I shall honor Thee
In humility

Even when difficult you find life
You must obey Jesus without strife
For your commander is He
The One with all authority
Your love you do prove
If to obedience, His will you does move
Empty don't let your love be
Living in vanity
For the Word is very clear
Obedience will bring the Savior cheer
Yes, in you He does delight
So with Christ don't put up a fight
When an order you hear
Obey in godly fear
Then the Spirit you will not grieve
And His presence will not leave

The love of Jesus we need
To handle our trials indeed
The courage is there
In the One Who for us does care
He can strengthen our hand
To endure trouble in the land
For if through the great tribulation we go
Our Savior we must thoroughly know
His voice we need to hear
And to us it must be clear
Scripture will be our guide
As in Christ we abide
To Him we must remain true
And trust the whole way through
Then if for Jesus we must die
Our faith let us never deny

Lord, thank You for things divine
Such as with Your will to align
Not only blessings does this bring
It brings joy and delight to my King
You see through my fears
That at times I obey almost with tears
But after Your will I have done
It's the most rewarding thing under the sun
So no longer will I delay
I'll listen after in faith I pray
My brothers I'll encourage to listen too
So as the Body we're faithful to you
To follow we all need His grace
For there are difficult times to face
They are already coming upon this earth
And they won't be in a dearth

Keepeth His word He always will do
Our Lord Jesus is forever faithful and true
It may be just in the nick of time
But nothing can thwart Christ sublime
His ability never doubt
For in power He is robust and stout
But He is gentle like a dove
So full of love
His mercy will never stop
As is shown in every precious blood drop
For Calvary is the deepest expression of compassion
Man never such could fashion
In the Lamb is found the best of all things
Such lovely reality He brings
Lord, I want to love Thee with all that is mine
Ever pleasing Christ divine

Only Christ can satisfy the hungry heart
He alone knows the healing art
So to Him I'll take my thirst
And learn to make Him always first
The living waters He pours out
The most refreshing without a doubt
As I deeply drink
How blessed am I, this I think
Every living soul He can satisfy
They must admit without Christ they are dry
He wants to be their source
But first they must admit they're off course
He will guide them back
If they take faith's track
So Lord, I can only pray
That You don't let any slip away

Learning Christ to follow
Eliminates all in life that is hollow
Real meaning is there
When for His will you care
It's a principle in life
That obedience rids your heart from strife
And in the fondest way
Christ to your heart this will say
Just keep an open ear
Then His wisdom you shall hear
It took many long years
For Christ to conquer my fears
But now I'm learning to trust
To be an overcomer this is a must
For my sisters and brothers I want the same
These dear ones who call upon Your name

Without resentment give
For that is the way Christ to live
Jesus always gave with a glad heart
With what was His He was not afraid to part
That was a sweet virtue of His humanity
Never did the Lord suffer from vanity
With Him the Father was pleased always
How He brightened the Father's days
He calls us to live likewise
The Father's will to prize
To us Christ will reveal it
In accordance with the Holy Writ
Good results it will yield
As we labor in God's field
A harvest to reap
Kingdom people for Christ to love and keep

Learning to listen to my Lord
The best growth does afford
His wisdom far exceeds mine
For His knowledge is divine
So I'll take the clue
And follow what He says to do
Much greater will be my joy
And much better my time I'll employ
Then a reward will await me
When my Lord Jesus I see
I know my Lord is kind
So His will pleasant I find
Procrastinate I must not do
But on His clear commands, promptly follow through
Then peace in my soul will pervade
And real progress will be made

Always loving is my King
Always over me He does sing
When I sin against Him
He's full of mercy to the brim
A grudge He will not hold
But invites me into His presence bold
How I want to be like Christ my Friend
And let all traces of bitterness end
How that would free my heart
For I want my personality pleasant, never tart
The Lord is the only One Who can bring this about
He will if I do not doubt
Belief makes the way
And gives confidence when I pray
So Lord, the life of faith I will live
For pleasure to Thee that does give

The Spirit wants to talk
About having a godly walk
Loose ends I would not leave
But to my Lord's will I'd cleave
He will prosper my soul
As I obey in the whole
Time and again
By faith I must avoid sin
But even more urgent for me
Is to love Jesus entirely
Every aspect of Him is good
This I know, as more of Him is understood
How pleasant I find my Friend
I hope our conversation never does end
And when in person I behold my Lord
I'll have the sweet knowledge that sight does afford

Lord, I want to keep my eyes on You
Not on what others do
Remind me of my own beam
So my brothers I would esteem
For all the sins that I have done
There's no reason I should be loved by God's Son
So Lord, grateful I will be
That You've forgiven me
My brothers I will build up
As together with Thee we sup
No right have I judgment to pass
Of me that is rather crass
All judgment belongs to our King
Only He can do the proper thing
So from my flesh I'll turn away
And in a loving spirit I'll stay

Jesus sits well with me
I have no reason not to fully love Thee
It's not for a lack of desire
But from some fear of being on fire
Somewhat lukewarm still am I
This I cannot deny
Lord, I need Thy mercy and grace
This lack in me to face
Overcome it I would like to do
Lord, help me depend on You
Precious time I know I am wasting
But of Your goodness I still am tasting
A "well done" someday I would like to hear
Please conquer my fear
More time I know it will take
I'll just persevere for Your glory's sake

The promises of this earth
Are nothing compared with those of the new birth
For those rooted in the Lord
The greatest pleasures do afford
Jesus is the fanciest feast
Never will these joys cease
As Jesus fills us with more love
How we'll long for the glories above
They will fill the hungriest heart
Especially when eternity does start
When the Lamb we behold
Our feelings will have no hint of being cold
Our hearts will melt
As His love is so strongly felt
Then the meaning of this verse we'll know
"God is love," as the Bible says so

The Lord is coming back soon
It could be midnight or noon
So be a bride made ready
Follow Jesus true and steady
Be obedient in things great and small
By grace giving your all
For Christ applied Himself in all that He did do
So we could be born anew
So His example take
From the moment you awake
Start the day with a turned heart
And from that stance don't depart
Then the Savior's voice will be clear
As your life He does steer
Then accomplish His purpose in you He shall
And your life will end so very well

Of grace there is a rich store
To draw from now and evermore
When a struggle or duty you face
Immediately come to the throne of grace
If your faith you exercise
Joy you will surely realize
Then to your effort there will be an ease
And Christ by faith you'll please
Harm the Lord does not want to bring
But life and peace of which to sing
Comfort your heart He shall
That is the way to be made well
You know joyful is our God
So you also on this path can trod
And Jesus will never deny
A soul who to Him for strength does cry
So just be at peace
And let your love for Him never cease

How important obedience is
If you claim to be His
An option it is not
If you want Christ to be inwrought
Don't consider His commandments to be too much
Their wisdom your heart will touch
Peaceable fruit they will yield
And put about you a shield
They will teach you how to love
Just like our Savior above
So rebellion overcome
Obey each edict, not just some
How this will please the Lamb
And be such praise to the Great I AM
So if necessary, do an about turn
And Christ's ways truly learn

The riches of this world are not my desire
But that one day my heart would be on fire
Christ would have first place
And I would always give grace
I would properly represent my King
In how I do everything
Mercy I would extend to others
Especially my sisters and brothers
Glory to Christ I would give alway
And magnify Him each day
Lofty goals these are
But from each believer they are not far
Faith and love can do it all
Even for children of the Fall
So Christ let us seek
And in faith never be weak

He's tender toward you and me
It's so plain to see
For salvation made it true
He could not any more love me or you
It's not like human love
But higher than the heavens above
It won't let us fail
Or problems us too hard assail
It is peaceful and sweet
Longing for us to be made complete
Prudent He is
Toward those who are His
Us He won't spoil
And He still lets us for our bread toil
But the salvation benefits He does give
Causes us like kings to live

To His goodness there is no upper bound
And His theology is perfectly sound
Since for us God did die
You know this is not a lie
And He proves it every day
In so many a way
By mercy that is complete
By a tender word so sweet
By meeting our physical needs
And many compassionate deeds
Putting joy in a heart that was sad
Being slow to get angry or mad
Giving justice to the weak
Displaying a heart that is meek
In ways that we cannot number
All day and night for Jesus does not slumber
His goodness appreciate do I
And to love Him, in grace I will comply

It's not what I think about me
But what my Lord Jesus does see
He knows my heart much better than I
The truth He will not deny
He sees the good and bad
Some things about me make Him glad
Other things cause Him concern
But His love in all I can discern
He will never condemn my soul
But labors to make me whole
So in His comfort I can find
Him always easing my mind
How precious is His love
Kindly sent from above
This Redeemer of mine
Is so fully divine

How grace the victory gives
For in my spirit Jesus lives
I have a supply divine
I can call mine
It overcomes trials
And causes joyful smiles
Of grace you can never speak enough
How it overcomes when times are rough
It's a privilege to have this source
Coming from Christ our course
Forever indebted am I
To my sweet Jesus on high
And He must always be first in my heart
With all idols I would part
For I know jealous is His name
So no other loves will I proclaim

Jesus is free
To love everybody
With sin He is not bound
His heart beats the sweetest sound
He cares for those the world does reject
On His heart they have a great effect
In them He sees beauty
With love, not a sense of duty
Even though He does not please all
He still deserves that souls on Him would call
He would like to make everyone God's child
From the rough to the mild
For this He needs our cooperation
That we would go to every nation
And proclaim the Good News
As for His glory, Christ us does use

I've been redeemed by love
That of my dear Jesus above
He shed His precious blood for me
And opened my eyes so Him I could see
I saw a Savior Who did care
And life with me He wanted to share
He wanted to rule in my life
And rid me of ugliness and strife
My sins I saw
And I was condemned by the law
But when I did repent
Seasons of refreshing were sent
To Him I did bow
And Jesus came in to dwell somehow
Explain it I could not
But by Him I was bought
Now my life is spent Jesus to gain
And to love this God, Who for me was slain

God you can trust
To flee youthful lust
A path He has made
With the price Christ has paid
Victory the cross does give
In holiness you can live
Let Christ capture your heart
With each new day you start
If your mind is set on Him
Life you'll know to the brim
Death it will swallow up
More so as with Jesus you sup
Then Jesus you will please
As you take up His yoke of ease
And rest you will find
With peace of mind

My Daddy loves me fore'er
As in Christ He does care
In Christ He expresses His heart
A relationship to start
He woos me each day
On His bosom to lay
There He will caress
As Abba I confess
My Father is fair like His Son
To Him I can always run
A bruised heart He will heal
As I enjoy with Him a spiritual meal
The Lamb I enjoy with my Father
Then troubles will no longer bother
I'm so glad the Triune God is mine
Father, Son, and Spirit all so fine

I'm feasting at the King's table
To make me glad He is well able
As He ponders His creation
Over the saved He has elation
Together we dine
And our delight is so fine
How praiseworthy is this time
In the presence of the sublime
And this is ours for aye
Enjoyment each glorious day
Chosen were we
To company with Thee
Fathom Your ways I cannot always do
But I know they are good and true
Lord, thank You for the mercy shown me
How I appreciate Thee

For self don't live
To others learn to give
A selfish life is dry
It will never satisfy
Take the example of our Lord
Who gave all His loving heart could afford
Self was not on His mind
To others He was invariably kind
He followed His Father's plan
He was the most gracious Man
When tired He still gave
Of Christ I must rave
Our God is tremendously good
By man He wants to be understood
His intentions are always in love
To draw man to things above

Wonderful and gentle are His ways
How can I not help but Jesus praise
His leading is never rough
His prodding is just enough
His will is strong
But with us He suffers long
To Him how can I say no
Not if I want my love to grow
That is surely my desire
Someday to be fully on fire
Lukewarm I don't want
But hot or cold you see
A well done I long to hear
And a Judgment Day without fear
So Lord, I will press on to higher ground
And truly faithful ever be found

Lord, feed me Your tender love
So I more fully enjoy my Savior above
O how heaven's King
Always makes me sing
Yes, He is righteous and just
But in His mercy I can trust
Advantage of Him I cannot take
I must follow for love's sake
He sets the boundary line
In a way that is fair and fine
I don't want to cross to the other side
But in His pleasure abide
For if His will I complete
Salvation will taste all the more sweet
And a reward I will pile up
On which to forever sup

A friend will always love
As does our Jesus above
He never withholds His heart
Not even a little part
In the cross He gave it all
Loving sinners of the Fall
His great desire
Was to snatch us from the fire
Now with us He does plead
To lovingly follow His lead
Then He has the way
To complete the sons of day
Apart from Him nothing can I do
I need His strength to follow through
Lord, cause me to trust in Your power
Starting this very hour

Learn to love every soul
For Jesus loves each one from pole to pole
Aloof don't be
For it does not glorify Thee
Friendly was our Lord
With all the kindness His heart could afford
With a crowd He would mix
Just loving, not making people a problem to fix
He knows we have many a flaw
But His sweetness sinners would draw
The Father He did please
Making people at ease
It was easy to converse with our God
He would comfort and guide with His staff and rod
So approach Him today
For He still has wonderful things to say

Show patience with others
Both unbelievers and brothers
Let Christ's forbearance be known
As to you it was shown
Display His grace
If hostility you must face
Draw on His unlimited love and power
To show mercy each hour
Never forget in the Lord to rejoice
If you want these virtues that must be your choice
For as we sup with Him
He fills us to the brim
Then your spirit will bubble over
Like the sweet fragrance of clover
And Christ will have the praise
As our voices to heaven we raise

For my forgiveness much gratitude I have
To my conscience it is a healing salve
The wall was broken down
Now by Christ I am found
Happy is my heart
That with God I have a brand new start
And if I slip and sin
Christ will forgive me each time again
He offers the same hope to all
They only need on Jesus to call
A Lord, Savior, and Friend He offers to be
Receive Him in faith's simplicity
Don't complicate the way
For a repenting heart do pray
Then open the door
With Christ to sup forevermore

Don't devour one another
For in Christ you are sister and brother
Learn to be gentle in all of your dealings
Not hurting each other's feelings
If a disagreement there is
Remember we are all His
So forbearance we need to show
Never causing a row
Kindness always seek
With a spirit that is meek
Don't worry about a brother's fault
Concentrate on Christ, Him to exalt
Then peace will be in your heart
And from your brother you won't want to part
The oneness of the Spirit keep
Then you won't lose any sleep

How the Lord loves a transformed soul
One that is becoming like Jesus, more whole
It is the Spirit's conforming
Not ourselves, on our own, reforming
When Jesus is added to our being
There is a wonderful work inside unseen
Our Christ it will show
As more of the divine life we know
Self will come to nothing
Making of Jesus something
For we want Him on display
Not the things we do and say
He is the center of attraction in this life
The One Who ends man's bitter strife
The more of Him we make
More of self-glory we'll forsake

Index

Edwards Brothers Malloy
Thorofare, NJ USA
January 23, 2015